D0834172

Siamese Cats – The Complete Care Guide to Siamese Cats

By Jess Carter

Foreword

Welcoming a Siamese Cat to your home is a wondrous experience. These truly unique creatures will bring so much joy to your lives. By understanding the history, biology and personality traits of the magnificent Siamese Cats, you will be able to be the best owner you can. Additionally, you will have a far greater appreciation and understanding of their exceptional qualities.

Siamese Cats differ greatly to all other breeds of cats. This is true for their distinctive appearance as well as their characteristic behavior. The bonds established between the Siamese Cat and their human owner are tremendous. Indeed, Siamese Cats are often regarded as similar to dogs – and perhaps even more accurately, to human children!

These cats are capable of so much and as an owner, be sure that you maximize the possibilities with your cat. As one of the most intelligent breeds of cats, you will be able to train your Siamese; play interactive games and walk them on a lead.

However, it is very important to note that with their incredibly inquisitive nature, Siamese Cats are both hugely rewarding – but also exceptionally demanding! Without adequate companionship and stimulation, your Siamese can become quite destructive. If you are considering

Foreword

introducing a Siamese cat to your home, make sure that you are ready – and that you have the time and inclination to meet their needs.

These fabulous cats require a high degree of maintenance. With this handbook at your side, you will be prepared and ready - to provide the very best home and care for your beloved pet.

This is the perfect read for people with a general love of Siamese Cats, prospective owners and also, for people who have owned Siamese Cats for some time. It is true to say that we gain so much from knowledge – and with this extra knowledge, we can give so much more to these truly deserving one of a kind cats.

Table of Contents

Table of Contents

Table of Contents

Table of Contents

Table of Contents

Chapter One - Introduction

Meet the Siamese Cat

With their beautiful and elegant appearance, Siamese cats are undoubtedly highly sophisticated. With strong personalities, these remarkable cats tend to be extrovert and extremely sociable. Strong bonds are formed between the cat and the owner. Siamese cats are virtually always highly loyal to their caregivers.

Siamese cats are known for their distinguished markings and pointed color patterns. They also have a distinctive head shape – almost triangular, it is often described as

Siamese Cats – The Complete Care Guide - Page 9

wedge shaped. The ears are prominent; large, pointed, and very wide at the base. Their dazzling blue eyes are slanted – shaped like almonds.

The body of the modern Siamese cat is long, muscular and very lean.

If asked to think about the appearance of a Siamese cat, the majority of people would conjure up the image of the modern Siamese – as just described. However, Siamese cats have not always looked this way – and more 'traditional' Siamese cats still exist today.

In looking at the history of the Siamese cat, we can understand how their looks and temperaments have developed, changed, and evolved. Over time, selected breeding has effectively led to the development of two distinct sub-breeds of Siamese cats.

Exploring History of the Siamese Cat

Without doubt, one of the most famous and popular cat breeds throughout the world, Siamese cats have a long and fascinating history.

The Siamese Cat is one of the original recognized breeds of Asian cat. The name Siamese stems from their origins – they originated in Siam – now known as Thailand.

Chapter One - Introduction

Historians have found a collection of ancient manuscripts called the Tamra Maew (meaning The Cat-Book Poems). Within these manuscripts there are descriptions and depictions of the Siamese Cat (known then in Siam as Wichienmaat). These manuscripts date back to the Ayutthaya Kingdom – between 1351 and 1767 AD.

As well as describing the original Siamese cat, the Tamra Maew also portrayed other heritage cats of Siam (Thailand). They include the Korat cat, the Konja cat (Black cat) and Suphalak. The Korat cat is still bred for preservation in Thailand today and have become popular in other countries as well.

In Thailand, Siamese cats are still called Wichien -maat. This is roughly translated to "Moon Diamond".

Burmese – Siamese War

The capital city of Ayutthaya was destroyed on the 7th April 1767. This marked the end of the Burmese – Siamese war. At this time, the Burmese army burned absolutely everything. Siamese noblemen and royal family members were captured and taken to Burma.

Legends Unfolded

There is a legend that the Burmese King (King Hsinbyushin), found and read the poem for the Thai cats in the Tamra Maew. In the poem, all Thai cats were described as being as rare as gold. The legend was that any person owning one of these Thai cats would become wealthy.

It is said that the King instructed his army to find and bring to him all the Suphalak cats (and all other treasure) where they would remain in Burma.

In Thailand, this legend is still told in a humorous way – the legend is said to explain why all Thai cats are so rare.

Siamese Cats Introduced to the West

It is thought that Siamese cats were first seen in the West in the late nineteenth century.

There are no documents to show when Siamese cats were first introduced to the United States of America. However, at least by the turn of the century, possibly even earlier than this, it is true to say that the Siamese cats had also become popular in the US. Probably due to their unique and sophisticated appearance, they were regarded as highly fashionable.

The first documented Siamese cat to arrive in America was a gift to the First Lady - Lucy Hayes, wife of President

Rutherford B. Hayes (1877 – 1881). Indeed, she received a Siamese cat as a gift in 1878. This rather remarkable gift was sent by David B. Sickels – a U.S. diplomat who as stationed at the consulate in Thailand.

In April 1909, the first Siamese Cat Society was formed in America.

Their first documented appearance is when they were formally exhibited at a Crystal Palace Cat Show in London.

The first documented appearance of Siamese cats in the United Kingdom was in 1884. This was when the British Consul-General in Bangkok, brought a breeding pair of the cats, Pho and Mia, to Britain. He presented them to his sister, Lilian Jane Gould as a gift.

These particular Siamese cats had been bred in the royal palace so were regarded as a truly magnificent and regal.

In 1885, Gould's cats, Pho and Mia, produced three kittens. They were named Duen Ngai, Kalohom, and Khromata. They were exhibited (both cats and kittens) at the Crystal Palace Cat Show, in London, in October 1885.

("The Book of the Cat" by Frances Simpson) [Public domain], via Wikimedia Commons

With their extraordinary appearance and strong characterful personalities, these Siamese cats made a huge impression. They were well photographed and very soon there was a surge in the popularity of Siamese cats in Britain.

At the beginning of their popularity, Siamese cats were named "The Royal Cat of Siam". This name seems to have emerged in response to stories that these cats had been exclusively kept be Siamese royalty. Further research has shown that there is no documentation or evidence of a Royal organized breeding program in Siam.

In 1902, the first Siamese cat fancier's club was formed in England.

Breeding

While the Siamese breed was gaining huge popularity in the U.S. and in the U.K, in Siam (now Thailand), very few people were breeding them.

In Western countries during the 1960's, breeders began to show preference for a different look to the Siamese cat. This effectively changed the appearance of the breed – to the elongated and lean Siamese cat that we are accustomed to today.

This breeding pattern has effectively established two sub-breeds of the Siamese cat – the traditional Siamese and the modern Siamese.

Traditional Siamese Cats

The original Siamese cats that were imported to the Western world were of medium size. They had a longish, muscular body. These cats had a moderately wedge-shaped head. Ears were rather large but in proportion to their head-size. These Siamese cats did not have 'extreme' features as can be said of the Modern Siamese cats.

By 1986, the cat shows were no longer exhibiting any traditional Siamese Cats. This was mainly in response to the massive popularity of the 'modern style'.

Many breeders stopped raising the traditional Siamese. Fortuitously however, some breeders continued raising the traditional style. This was out of a personal preference - in spite of the fact that the traditional Siamese were widely seen as 'inferior' and less fashionable.

Additionally, several organizations formed to preserve and protect this traditional sub-breed. These organizations arranged shows and opportunities to exhibit their beloved cats. Today, the traditional Siamese cat is well established and seems set to continue thriving.

The original Siamese cats had tails with 'kinks' in them. Through breeding, these 'kinks' in the tail are now extremely rare. However, in Thailand, there are many Siamese street cats that have short and kinked tails. This is a clear illustration of how human intervention and breeding has affected evolution.

The Tale of the Kinked Tail

There are several traditional stories that conjecture why the Siamese had a kink in their tail.

The following is an example of one such tail.

Once upon a time, inside a beautiful Siamese Temple, an exquisite royal goblet went missing.

The King ordered all of his people to search for the missing goblet. As part of the search, a young couple and their cat went into the jungle. Here they found the golden goblet. Unfortunately, the goblet was so heavy that they were not able to carry it back to the Temple.

While the young man returned to the temple to tell of their find, the young lady and the cat stayed with the golden goblet.

The cat took guard of the goblet, wrapping his tail around the stem of the goblet to provide protection.

The young man returned with the priest from the temple four days later. Here they found the cat with her tail still around the goblet – and five delightful kittens.

It is believed that the cat was so sincere about the safety of the goblet, that a permanent kink developed at the end of his tail. Surprisingly, all five kittens had a kink in their tail too!

As the popularity of the traditional Siamese cat increases, it is always possible that breeders will begin to favor 'kinks' in the tail again - they may yet make a comeback! Afterall, the kinked tail is still commonly seen among street cats in Thailand.

Modern Siamese Cats

When people are told to think of a Siamese cat, they will generally conjure up a very typical image.

This will be of a cat with a perfect wedge shaped (or triangular) head. With a pronounced underlying bone structure, the head is very narrow.

Eyes are dazzling blue, slanted and almond shaped. The ears are a dominating feature – very large in proportion to the head size, pointed and wide set.

Bodies are remarkably elongated, both lean and muscular. The tail is very long and very thin, narrowing, very gradually to a point.

This image is that of the modern Siamese cat. It is the result of selective breeding. Indeed, during the 1950's and 1960's, most breeders and cat show judges began to favor the slenderer look.

Types of Siamese Cats

Resulting from selective breeding, there are now effectively three types of Siamese cat;

- The Traditional Siamese. Although not officially, these are also referred to as 'Old-Style Siamese', and 'Appleheads'. The term 'Applehead' began as a disparaging phrase. It was adopted by breeders of the modern style Siamese who they considered as superior, and the traditional as inferior.
- The Classic Siamese. This is essentially a cross between the other two types, without the extremes.

The classic is sometimes named as the 'Old-Style' which makes reference to the fact that this is the type that was most common in the 1950's, 1960's and 1970's.

The Classic Siamese are medium sized, slender but muscular. They have a moderate wedge-shaped head and face. Indeed, there is more definition to the muzzle compared to the traditional, but it is not extreme like the modern.

The legs of the Classic Siamese are longer than the Traditional, but not as long as the Modern.

They have a long, thin and tapered tail.

- The Modern Siamese. Also known as the 'Show Style' and 'standardized' – and Wedgehead or Extreme Wedgehead.

The Modern Siamese is the latest of the Siamese types and it is the current preference in cat shows and registries today.

Every type of this type's appearance is extreme. They are extremely svelte, lithe and muscular – but fined boned and slender all over.

The head is an extreme wedge shape, forming a sharp triangle from chin to the tip of the ears. Compared to the classic, they have longer muzzles. Their ears are very large in proportion to the rest of the head. The head size is smaller in the Modern Siamese.

They have very long slim legs and an exceptionally long tapered tail (longer than the Classic and Traditional).

Although both the traditional and modern Siamese descended from the same distant ancestors, they had few or no recent ancestors in common. This explains why they are commonly considered as three different sub-breeds. Some may argue that they should be considered as three distinct breeds altogether.

The Siamese are recognized by all cat associations. The International Cat Association and the World Cat Federation now accept Siamese cats of the less extreme type – and any *Wichianmat* cat that is imported directly from Thailand. These are classified under the new breed name – 'Thai'.

Crossbreeding

Siamese cats (both traditional and modern) are among the foundation stock of several other breeds that have been developed by crossbreeding Siamese with other cats.

These include the Balinese, Oriental, The Himalayan division of the Persian, the Tonkinese and the Havana Brown.

The Oriental Shorthair was developed to extend the range of coat patterns. The Himalayan is a longhaired variant.

Chapter Two – Physical Characteristics

Knowing the historical background to these cats, it is fascinating to look more closely at their beautiful physical features.

Wedge Shaped Head

Siamese cats have both an alert and intelligent expression.

The breed standard of the modern Siamese calls for a triangular / wedge shaped head. The head is long, neither rounded or pointed. There should be a perfect triangle from the tip of the nose to the tip of each ear.

In the face, the underlying bone structure is very pronounced. This is especially true when the whiskers are smoothed back.

Their remarkably large ears are wide at the base and pointed at the tip. This gives them the same triangular shape as the head.

Siamese cats have intensely blue eyes. These are slanted towards the nose and are almond shaped.

Slender Bodied

The modern Siamese cats have longer and leaner bodies than their traditional counterparts. Breeders have effectively developed extremely muscular bodies that are both lean and elongated.

Indeed, Siamese cats are prized for their athletic appearance and also for their extraordinarily graceful movements.

The Siamese cat has long and lean legs with small, oval shaped paws. The hind legs are higher than the front legs.

The neck is both long and graceful.

The tail is long and tapering, gradually ending in an elegant point.

The Siamese Coat and Points

The short coat of the Siamese cat is glossy and fine.

Siamese kittens are born either pure cream or a brilliant white. At around four weeks of age, their true colors finally emerge!

Coloring is bizarrely the result of a genetic mutation. Indeed, the distinctive pointed pattern is a form of partial albinism.

This genetic mutation means that the production of melanin (the body's natural skin pigment) fails to work at normal body temperatures.

This effectively means that the cooler areas of the body – including the extremities (for example, legs, feet, ears, tail) and the face become a darker color. The face is a cooler part of the body as it is cooled by the passage of air that passes through the sinuses.

This has resulted in the famous 'pointed' coat pattern that helps to make the Siamese cats stand out.

By the time a kitten is four weeks old, the points tend to be sufficiently noticeable so that their coloring can be identified.

With age, Siamese cats tend to darken. Also, adult Siamese living in warmer climates are more likely to be lighter in color than those in cooler places.

Pointed Color Scheme

Originally, the majority of Siamese cats had seal point colorings. These are extremely dark brown, almost black.

Over time, other colors began to emerge. Sometimes, kittens were born with different colored points.

These new colors were originally regarded as inferior seal points. They were not considered as qualified for showing or breeding.

Gradually, these shades became accepted by the breed associations. Once accepted, these colorings became more widespread due to breeding programs which were specifically designed to produce these colors.

Color variations include;

- 'Seal Point'. The points are extremely dark brown, with dark brown nose and paw pads. The body is pale fawn to cream.
- 'Blue Point' – The body is white with a slight blue hue. Points are of a cool gray coloring and nose and paw pads a slate color. Genetically, this is a dilution of seal point.
- 'Chocolate' – The body is ivory colored with light brown (milk chocolate) colored points. Nose and paw pads are pink. This is a genetic variation of the original seal points.
- 'Lilac' – A white body with pink / warm shade of gray points. Nose and paw pads are pink. Genetically, this is a diluted chocolate.

In the United States, a major cat registry, the Cat Fanciers' Association, considers only these four original colors as Siamese – seal point, blue point, chocolate point, and lilac point.

However, the International Cat Association accepts a range of colors beyond the four that are recognized by the Cat Fanciers' Association of the U.S.

Outcrossing with other breeds has led to Siamese-mix cats that have points in other cat colors and patterns! These colors include Lynx (tabby) point, Red and Cream point, and Tortoise-shell point. Whilst the UK and other countries consider these variations to be all part of the Siamese breed, the U.S. excludes them.

Interestingly, in the U.S., Oriental Shorthair cats with color points in other colors or patterns (in addition to these four), are accepted (in the registry of the Cat Fanciers' Association). The World Cat Federation also uses this classification – effectively treating the Oriental Shorthair as a separate breed.

Chapter Three – Exploring Common Perceptions

Perhaps in part due to their stunning appearance, Siamese cats tend to have a rather stereotypical image. This is, of course, only by people who have not been fortunate enough to have contact with - and get to know these gorgeous creatures.

Challenging the Stereotype

The stereotypical representation of the Siamese cat is inclined to be of a cat that is aloof, mysterious, downright unfriendly and even rather sinister in nature. This is unquestionably inaccurate, wrong and misleading!

For any of you readers who have already had any kind of contact with a Siamese cat, you will know that this could not be further from the truth. For you readers who have not yet met a Siamese cat, you are in for an absolute treat! Undeniably, Siamese cats are anything but aloof and mysterious.

So, where do these stereotypes originate from?

Siamese Cats in the Movies

This misunderstanding is most likely influenced by the unreasonable portrayal of the Siamese cats in the Disney's 1995 blockbuster movie, 'The Lady and the Tramp'.

In this movie, the pair of Siamese cats, Si and Am, peek out from a picnic basket giving a truly sinister impression – eyes glowing fiery blue and long tails swishing menacingly. Lady (the Cocker spaniel heroine) feels threatened by the two Siamese cats.

The pair then emerge in perfect synchronization and begin to sing their ill-famed song, "The Siamese Cat Song". The cats are shown to look at Lady in a highly intimidating fashion – looking at her as if they wanted to either devour her or simply use her as a toy.

The 'sinister' pair do not care about anyone or anything else – causing havoc and distress – stalking the goldfish, running up the drapes, destroying the furniture and then laying all the blame on Lady.

In Roald Dahl's Charlie and the Chocolate Factory, the Oompa Loompa Song includes the words, "Who do you blame when your kid is a brat? / Pampered and spoiled like a Siamese cat."

A Siamese cat played a prominent role in the 1958 movie 'Bell, Book and Candle'. The Siamese, named Pyewacket, helps to cast spells with his owner, who is a witch. Pyewacket is extraordinarily bewitching, verging on sinister.

The 1965 movie, 'That Darn Cat', features a traditional Siamese cat, D.C, who is mischievous through and through. Involved in many escapades, D.C has an attitude and an inclination to roam.

These movies give a very one-dimensional view of the Siamese cat. They tend to be judged based on their elegant appearance and are assumed to be aloof and independent – even without love and affection. This is an unfair and inaccurate portrayal - but fortunately, you and I are privileged enough to know much better.

Character Traits

While Siamese cats are often portrayed as aloof (arguably more so in comparison to other breeds of cats), they are incredibly social creatures – bizarrely, more so than other cat breeds. Siamese cats often exhibit extrovert personalities – and tend to be extraordinarily sociable.

In the following chapter, we will look at the behavior and personalities of Siamese cats in greater depth. But for now, we know enough to dispel the myth that Siamese cats are aloof and detached. Indeed, Siamese cats are usually incredibly affectionate.

Loud!

Siamese cats are known to be highly vocal and this one isn't just a stereotype! The clear majority of Siamese cats are extremely 'talkative', making their wishes and demands known through a series of meowing.

The meow of the Siamese cat is sometimes compared to that of a crying human baby. This is most likely due to the type of sound as well as the intense volume both a Siamese cat and a human baby can make! Oftentimes, a Siamese cat can sound like they are in severe pain when they are just talking and are actually just fine!

I talk in greater detail about the Siamese cat's tendency to be talkative in the following chapter under the section 'Highly Vocal'.

A Tendency for Trouble

It is probably true to say that Siamese cats have a slight tendency towards trouble-making. This is probably in consequence of their high intelligence.

By nature, Siamese cats are very inquisitive. They will be keen to open doors, cabinets and latches – all part of exploring the world they live in.

Indeed, in preparation for your new Siamese cat, it would be sensible to "cat-proof" your home. Make sure you find ways to secure doors and cupboards that you do not wish your Siamese cat to nose around in.

Owning a Siamese cat comes hand in hand with being amazed at what trouble they can get into! It seems that they get a huge degree of satisfaction from finding creative and remarkable ways to get into trouble. You will be kept busy (although hopefully, in part amused), trying to put a stop to some of their antics!

Dominant Personalities

With humans, a Siamese cat will be nothing but loyal and
devoted. However, they do tend to have extraordinarily
dominant personalities – and often take charge of the entire
household.

Siamese cats can be aggressive and territorial, particularly towards another cat (or cats) both within and outside of the household. This is discussed in greater detail in the next chapter, under 'aggression and domination'.

Chapter Four – Exploring Siamese Cat Behavior

It is undeniable that Siamese cats are unique. This is true of their appearance but equally true of their behavior. As well as being generally interesting, it is important to be aware of some of the unusual behaviors and character traits that are common within Siamese cats. This is particularly vital for all prospective Siamese cat owners – especially those that have not had direct contact with a Siamese cat before.

Siamese cats continuously exhibit behavior that is remarkably different to other feline counterparts. Indeed, Siamese cats display much more exaggerated behavior than is seen in other cats. They have a limitless abundance of affection to give to their owner. Concurrently, they can be highly disagreeable – aggressive towards other cats and extremely territorial – to both people and home.

In this chapter, we will explore the truths of Siamese cats.

Incredibly Sociable and Deeply Loyal

Not only can we dispel the myth that Siamese cats are aloof, but these one of a kind cats also show themselves to be highly sociable and fiercely loyal companions.

Chapter Four – Exploring Siamese Cat Behavior

Siamese cats tend not to be quite as independent as other breeds of cats. They form very close bonds with their human owners and rely on them for company.

Like nothing else, they love to be snuggled on your lap, beside you at bedtime and even joining you for mealtimes. Siamese cats tend to follow their owners around the home, watching their every move – and providing a commentary full of noisy meowing!

The social aspect of the Siamese cat makes them so demanding as a pet. They want to be a big part of your life – and they will make sure that they are just that.

Siamese cats enjoy the company of their owners to such an extent that they do not like to be left on their own for long periods of time.

If you are busy at work, it may be worth considering keeping two Siamese cats so that they have each other for company. If you are away for long periods of time, another cat breed may be a more sensible choice for you.

The Siamese cat is one that requires a lot of attention as well as stimulation. Without adequate attention, Siamese cats will usually howl or become destructive in the home.

Due to their highly sociable nature, the Siamese cats are rather high maintenance. This is especially true in comparison to other breeds of cat.

So, if you are thinking about welcoming a Siamese to your household, just be sure this is what you are looking for.

Perfect if you are looking for a loyal creature that will enjoy interacting and spending lots of time with you. Conversely, if you are looking for an independent pet – where you can carry out your busy life and not worry too much about being a companion to your pet, then the Siamese cat may not be the best choice for you.

Temperament

Whilst the Siamese cat is notably loving and affectionate, there is a significant flip side of this trait. This attribute tends to be unique to the Siamese cat – and is certainly worth considering.

Indeed, Siamese cats tend to exhibit quite a pronounced jealous aspect. While the Siamese cat will lap up attention and affection from family and friends, the Siamese is likely to be forceful if the attention craved is not provided.

The significance of this jealous trait is really dependent on the household where the Siamese cat will live. If people are around to provide attention, then this trait will not be a problem. If there are other cats or dogs – or young children which may be that the Siamese feels left out, then it can become a serious issue. The jealous trait really can lead to some seriously negative behavior.

Highly Vocal

Another trait that marks the Siamese cat apart from other cat breeds is their tendency to be tremendously vocal.

The majority of Siamese cats will vocalize – almost constantly –not simply when demanding something – but conversationally – throughout the day, expressing an opinion on everything!

Be aware that the Siamese cat tends to vocalize in a way that is much louder than other cat breeds. It can be that they sound like they are in a lot of pain – when they are actually merely conversing – this is perfectly normal!

Ultra-loud vocalizations tend to be reserved for when the Siamese cat needs / wants something from you. If you are able to respond to what it is they are asking for, then the intense vocalization will not be prolonged.

Siamese cats meow <u>a lot</u>, they like you to know what they are thinking about everything! If you are looking for a quiet life with a peaceful cat, perhaps the Siamese cat is not what you are looking for!

Insatiable need to Scratch

It is important for prospective owners to be aware that Siamese cats (as with all other cats) have an inevitable and insatiable need to scratch.

One option is of course declawing the cat. But in case this is not an option for you, this behavior issue is one to consider.

It is not appropriate to punish as it is such natural behavior – the cat has an instinctive need to sharpen those claws.

It is probably true to say that you will never eliminate scratching – but you can try and minimize it. This may be achieved by providing a scratch post or scratch pad – when your Siamese cat goes to scratch your carpet or furniture,

Siamese Cats – The Complete Care Guide - Page 42

you will be able to redirect them to the designated scratching area.

Aggression and Domination

Another personality trait of the Siamese cat is their instinct to be domineering. This perhaps ties in with their tendency to be jealous – they are so determined to be at the center, receiving all the attention – that they will dominate over other animals to ensure that they receive all possible attention.

With an abundance of attention and by keeping your Siamese cat busy and occupied, it might be that they tolerate another cat in the house – but they do like to make it known to all concerned that they are the cat in charge; the dominant character no question.

In a later chapter, we discuss ways to introduce your new Siamese cat to the rest of the household – including to children and other pets. (see Chapter Nine – Introducing your Siamese Cat).

The Siamese cat will be very aggressive in establishing their territory outside of the home– they will absolutely ensure that they are the dominant cat in their neighborhood – and will display very aggressive behavior to any cat that stands in their way.

If a Siamese cat is introduced to a household with other cats, it is pretty much always the Siamese cat that will end up dominating.

Decidedly Intelligent

All cats are inquisitive. They have an innate tendency to be curious, to explore and discover. Siamese cats are one of the most intelligent breeds of cat.

While following you around everywhere and chatting to you, your Siamese cat will also be watching everything that you do, learning as they go.

Siamese cats need to be stimulated. Otherwise, they tend to become bored and this is when they are likely to be troublesome. Interacting with your cat is the best kind of stimulation. They do like toys - as well as regular household items – they can be fascinated by something as basic as a tissue box or a toilet paper roll.

A Siamese cat will enjoy finding ways to open cupboards, doors and latches. Generally, if they decide they want to do something, they will do whatever they can to make sure they do it.

This means that you will need to Siamese cat proof your home – this is true for Siamese cats as well as Siamese kittens. You need to make sure that your home is a safe place for your cat – and ensure that your Siamese cat cannot cause too much damage to your home.

Siamese cats tend to remain inquisitive and playful, even as older cats.

Due to their high level of intelligence, it is possible and rewarding to train a Siamese cat. However, be aware that Siamese cats can also be stubborn – and may not always cooperate in your training program.

Innate Predators

Like other felines, Siamese cats are predators. Although all cats have an innate hunting and chasing instinct, this natural inclination to hunt and chase is very strong and noticeable within Siamese cats.

To be a successful predator, the cat needs very keen senses; stealth; rapid reactions; patience; caution; and the ability to learn from experiences. Cats are very adept at all of these skills.

Siamese cats within the home are keen to use these skills – regardless of the fact that there is no prey to chase indoors! This means that your beloved Siamese will likely pretend that people are prey – and play at attacking them. This will include pouncing on feet (especially any wiggly toes), chasing prey that is really not there – running up and down the stairs, up and down the drapes and chasing across tabletops. This inevitably generates a degree of chaos – something that prospective owners need to be prepared for.

Although you will not (and should not try) to eliminate this behavior, you can calm things down a little. Your Siamese cat will be stimulated by play. By playing and interacting with your Siamese; and using different types of toys to keep them interested and occupied, they will be calmer and far less destructive.

Additionally, scratch posts and scratch pads can be really helpful – proving a mini playground for your Siamese cat. You will also have a designated place where you can encourage your cat to scratch. After all, all cats need an outlet for scratching and sharpening their claws (see

Chapter Four – Exploring Siamese Cat Behavior
Chapter Ten – Bonding with your Siamese, Scratch Posts- a Necessity).

Chapter Five - Language and Communication

A huge part of the Siamese cat personality is their incredibly talkative nature. Highly opiniated, they will tell you what they think about everything.

Learning and understanding the language of your Siamese cat involves both body language and vocal cat sounds. With experience and the following tips that we share with you, you will be able to understand some of your cat's body language and vocalization.

You will experience a greater level of appreciation and form an even stronger bond by understanding what your Siamese cat is trying to communicate to you.

Interpreting Body Language

Much of what your Siamese cat says to you can be understood through an enhanced comprehension of their body language. This understanding will be greater the more time you spend with your Siamese cat.

- **Friendly body language** – When a Siamese cat is being friendly, their face will have an open expression.

Look at the ears and whiskers – they will both be pointed forwards. The body will be relaxed and the tail pointing straight upwards.

- **Trust and Friendship** – If you notice that your Siamese cat is looking at you and blinking very slowly, this is a sure sign of trust and friendship. Siamese cats, as well as other breeds, will do a slow blink, both to other cats and their humans, as a way of expressing their love.

To initiate this behavior, try looking into the eyes of your Siamese cat. Come down to the same level as your beloved companion and do some slow blinks. Allow some time, but it is very likely that your cat will respond with some slow blinks of their own!

- **An Aggressive Challenge** – Your Siamese cat will express an aggressive challenge to something / somebody – most likely another cat with some distinctive body language.

This includes staring eyes where the pupils are contracted. Ears will be upwards and turned back. Head and tail will be extended, and the body held firm, and inflexible.

- **Ready to Attack** – Signs that your Siamese cat is about to attack include a bushy tail and hair being raised along the back spine.

  Evolution can help explain why cats 'bush up' their fur before an attack. It is actually a defense mechanism and is used to make the cat appear larger – more aggressive and intimidating.

  When you witness this behavior, note that your Siamese cat will no longer respond to you rationally. Indeed, it is often the case that the cat will be so absorbed in anger and so focused on attack, that at this point, they would not even recognize their human owner. In this situation, the cat is responding and acting on its own instincts.

  The best way to break up a confrontation of this kind is by trying to break the spell of anger. Trying to make a loud noise, use a water squirter - or try placing a pillow, blanket or even coat between the two cats involved in the confrontation. If can bring your Siamese cat back to their senses, you will be able to avoid a physical confrontation and fight.

- **Submissive** – Where a cat is feeling submissive, other distinguishing body language is displayed.

Chapter Five - Language and Communication

The cat will flatten their ears to the side of the head. You will notice that pupils are dilated.

Often, the cat will crouch down or even roll over – this is for protection against an imminent attack.

The Language of Whiskers

Although perhaps not intentionally, your cat also communicates through their whiskers.

Indeed, when a cat is feeling playful and inquisitive, the whiskers will always be pointing forward and spread out. This is true when a cat is out hunting – or playing at hunting with a toy in the home. When a cat is feeling relaxed and neutral, whiskers will be pointing directly outwards and significantly less spread out. Conversely, when a cat is feeling frightened or nervous, whiskers will be lying flat on the cat's face.

Cat Grooming

Grooming between cats is genuine expression of friendliness and is used as a way of bonding and articulating affection.

This behavior begins when the cat is just a kitten. Mother cats lick their kittens from the very moment they are born. Grooming serves to remove all the debris and fluids that come about during birth. It also helps to stimulate the kittens breathing.

This early experience means that grooming becomes an instinctive behavior – one that expresses a bond between two cats or between cat and owner. It seems to represent the cat wishing to take care / look after either another cat or their owner.

Understanding Cat Talk

There are multiple different types of cat sounds. Research shows that cat vocalizations can be divided into three distinct groups – murmur patterns, vowel patterns, and strained-intensity sounds.

- **Murmurs** – These murmur patterns include all kind of vocalizations where the cat has their mouth closed – purring is a type of murmur as a purring occurs with the mouth closed.

  These type of cat sounds are generally expressions of friendliness and contentment.

- **Vowel Patterns** – The vowel sounds comprise of the 'conversational vocalizing' that all cats do. But Siamese are particularly loud with their vowel sounds – and make continuous use of them! Indeed, it seems true that most other Oriental cats are also particularly talkative – although I believe, none more so than our beloved Siamese.

  Most of these vocalizations are greetings, requests, demands, denials and frustrations.

Chapter Five - Language and Communication

You will notice that your Siamese cat loves it if you take the time to join in with their conversation and talk back to them.

- **Strained Intensity Sounds** – These sounds include hisses, growls, and screams that are used during attack and defense.

  You will notice that your Siamese cat will often "chatter" when watching a bird through a glass window. This sound results from a combination of lip-smacking and teeth chattering – and some squeaking!

  Strained intensity sounds also include sounds that are used during mating.

  The sound of a female cat in heat (particularly prominent in Siamese cats), can sound like a human baby crying. It is a very loud call – and the sound really can travel a very long way! The male also calls when the female is in heat – making a high-pitched song like sound.

Chapter Six – The Five Senses

Although the five senses are not unique to Siamese cats, they lie at the heart of every cat. To appreciate a cat's magnificence and special qualities, it is essential to consider their five senses – and how their senses affect their behavior and personality.

Indeed, cats have acute hearing and sight. Long whiskers protruding from the head and body enhance the cat's sense of touch. Cats have excellent night vision. These senses are what enables cats to hunt so effectively – particularly in darkness.

Sight and Superior Night Vision

Whilst cats have a far superior night vision in comparison to humans, cats are unable to see in complete darkness.

Like dogs and many other animals, cats have a *tapetum lucidum*. This is a reflective layer that sits behind the retina. It sends light that passes through the retina back into the eye. This makes very efficient use of the light available. This effectively means that cats are able to see very clearly in dim lighting – they only need one-sixth of the light we need to see.

In a cat's eye, the muscles of the iris surrounding the pupil are designed so that the eye narrows to a vertical slit in bright light – and opens fully in very dim light. This allows for maximum illumination.

It is the reflective layer behind the retina that makes the cat's eyes look like they are glowing when light is reflected from them. Whereas most cat breeds have eyes that appear greenish or golden when light is reflected from them, the eyes of the Siamese cat reflect a luminous red.

Although cats have far superior night vision, vision in the daylight is comparatively poor. In ordinary daylight, if perfect human vision is 20/20, then the vision of a cat is about 20/100. Whilst cats can see objects far away, up close vision is blurred.

You may have heard rumors that cats are colorblind. This is in fact, not true. Cats can see some colors – although their color vision is far inferior to that of a human.

The vision of the cat is clearly linked with survival – wild cats are nocturnal where hunting would be a nighttime activity. This is exactly what the eyesight of the cat is designed for.

Keen Sense of Smell

The average cat has a sense of smell that is about fourteen times stronger than that of a human. Cats rely on smell and scents to understand and interpret the world around them.

It is the cat's sense of smell that is used to communicate with other cats – and to establish territories and boundary lines.

Interestingly, cats have a special sense organ in the roof of their mouths. This is called the *Jacobson's organ*. It effectively allows them to *taste* scent molecules. This is a huge enhancement for their sense of smell.

Cats have such an acute sense of smell that they are aware of any animals that may be outside your home. They can also identify any smell of an animal that you have on your clothes from an earlier encounter.

This incredible sense of smell is what enables cats to establish boundaries and territories. Cats mark their territory by urinating and rubbing skin secretions on significant objects in their surroundings.

Remarkably, cats also use their sense of smell to test out and essentially taste the food you provide them.

Incredible Hearing

The hearing of a cat is truly remarkable.

The outer ear is controlled by 30 different muscles which means that they can rotate, almost like a miniature satellite dish! Sounds are picked up by the outer ear and then funneled into the inner ear and brain.

Each ear can be rotated 180 degrees and one or both ears can be positioned in the direction of sound. This enables cats to accurately pinpoint particular sounds.

Cats can also hear much higher frequencies than what humans can. This explains why cats are so adept at finding rodents – many sounds made by rodents cannot be picked up by the human ear – but they are loud and clear to a cat.

Interestingly, kittens make ultrasonic vocalizations that cannot be heard by humans – but guarantees that they will be heard by their Mum.

Cats are able to localize specific sounds. For example, a cat could differentiate different sounds that are about three feet away – where the sources are only three inches apart.

This ability to hear is also what makes cats such fierce and effective hunters. Indeed, cats can detect specific vibrations (such as ultrasonic sounds of rodents) in a very busy street.

Fascinating Sense of Touch

Most important to a cat, in terms of touch, is their whiskers. These are effectively touch receptors. Cats have a collection of special whiskers which are known as vibrissae. Cats have about 24 vibrissae which the cat can move. These are most prominent on either side of its nose and upper lip. They also have vibrissae on each cheek, over the eyes, on the chin, and on the legs.

Compared to ordinary hairs, vibrissae are much thicker. Their roots are full of nerve endings which are set within the cat's tissue.

Whiskers provide cats with a powerful sense of touch that helps them to understand the world they are living in. Whiskers provide information about air movements, air pressure, vibrations, and anything that their whiskers come into contact with.

Because whiskers can recognize tiny shifts in air currents, the cat is able to detect objects which are near to them – without actually needing to see them!

So, vibrissae are effectively used to enhance vision – through touch. Cats use their whiskers in the same way that we use the touch receptors in our finger tips – to feel our way around in the dark and to warn us of any potential danger.

As the cat's whiskers are as wide as it's body, cats can use them to determine whether they can fit into an entrance, hole or small space. They are essential for effective hunting and are actually also used to detect scents.

You will notice that your cat will find it difficult to drink or feed from a bowl where the whiskers touch the side of the bowl. This is because the whiskers that are touching the bowl will be sending sensations to their brain – making it difficult to focus on eating or drinking! To avoid this, check that the bowl is large enough so that your cat's whiskers are not rubbing on the sides of the dish.

Taste – the Weakest Link

Taste may well be the one sense that humans are superior in. A cat has 473 taste buds on their tongue – compare this to the human tongue which has approximately 9,000 taste buds!

As opposed to enjoying the taste of food, cats really appreciate food through smell. This explains the feline tendency to sniff food – and frequently walk away without so much as a taste. This is the *Jacobson's organ* in the roof of the cat's mouth that is at work – allowing your cat to essentially taste scent molecules.

However, as well as tasting the smell, the texture and temperature of the food will be important to your cat. Ordinarily, cats do not like food that is below room temperature – so it is not a good idea to store kitty food in the refrigerator. Their aversion to cold food is most likely connected to life in the wild. Indeed, non-domesticated cats would consume freshly killed prey – which is always still warm.

Cats can sometimes be encouraged to eat if food is warmed up slightly – by warming the food, the smell becomes stronger and more closely imitates freshly killed prey.

Chapter Seven – Choosing your Siamese Cat

Our 'Introduction' to Siamese cats may have helped you decide which kind of Siamese cat you would prefer. Indeed, knowing their personality traits and distinct behavior, you may feel committed and ready to proceed to ownership.

But before then, there are some basic realities to consider. This inevitably includes deciding where you will get your Siamese cat from; choosing male or female; and making practical preparations at home.

Choosing an Animal Shelter

Adopting a Siamese cat from an Animal Shelter can mean that you are giving a very deserving Siamese cat a second chance in life. Although it is impossible to offer a home with love and attention to all Siamese cats in shelters, adoption makes it possible to make the world of difference to one or two very special Siamese cats.

All animals, including Siamese cats, end up in an animal shelter for a whole host of reasons. It may be due to poor health or illness of previous owner, family break-up, change of home where it is no longer viable to keep pets, owners unable to meet needs of their Siamese due to work or other commitments. Some shelters also team up with rescue centers in the Middle East (places such as Qatar, Kuwait, Egypt) where purebred cats are frequently dumped on the street.

Whilst there are many reasons why a cat ends up in a rescue center, it is certainly not the case that there is usually a problem with the cat. A minority may have experienced neglect or abuse – but most of these cats will adjust and adapt to their new home providing they are given the love and care that they deserve.

You can be absolutely sure that you will save money if you are able to adopt from a Shelter. Additionally, shelters tend to microchip, spay, neuter and vaccinate the animals that come into their care. As well as saving you money, you will have the satisfaction that your Siamese will have had any health problems dealt with already.

It is in the interest of the Animal Shelter (not to mention the Siamese and yourself) to make sure that the Siamese you adopt will be a suitable member of your household. They will assess the personality of the Siamese who they will have spent time getting to know – to see what kind of home environment and owner it would be suited to. This means that the staff will be able to give you an idea of the Siamese cat's temperament and personality. They will also be aware of any behavioral difficulties.

This process explains why it can seem like a lengthy process when adopting through an Animal Shelter. To try and find the best home for their Siamese, staff will be looking for suitable matches – they will need to find out about you and your household – and will then find a Siamese that would be well suited to your home situation.

However, adopting a Siamese from an animal shelter may never be the best choice for everybody. If you would like a cat quickly; if you are specific about age and look; or you do not have time to deal with potential issues that may arise, it may be better to buy your cat through a breeder.

Finding the Right Breeder

All good breeders will love and be attached to their Siamese cats – both cats and kittens. They will be able to provide you with information about the breed. Crucially, good breeders will be committed to producing healthy kittens that are well socialized.

Be sure to visit the breeder and see for yourself that the premises are clean and well ordered.

Note that the breeder may ask you many questions. This shows that the breeder cares about the future of the kitten. Indeed, the breeder will be checking that the home you offer and the lifestyle you lead is suitable for a Siamese cat.

When you go to visit the kitten available for sale, be sure to ask to also see the 'Mama' cat and any other relatives. This may give you an indication of the temperament of the young kitten.

Feel free to ask the breeder as many questions as you can think of.

Find out where the kitten has been kept. Ideally, they have spent their first weeks in the home – this will mean that they are familiar with the noise and hustle and bustle of day-to-day domestic life. Generally, kittens that have been bought up in a breeder's home will settle into a new home with little upset and over a short time.

Ensure that you ask the breeder what they have done to socialize the kitten. It is important that they have spent time with the kitten so that it is accustomed to human interaction. If the kitten has not been properly socialized, it will find it difficult to interact with humans – and there is a far greater chance of behavioral problems.

Signs of a Healthy Siamese

When the exciting time arrives, and you are ready to choose your Siamese cat, you need to be aware of the signs that indicate good or poor health. Above all else, you want to bring home a cat that is in good health.

Sounds obvious - but do avoid picking out a cat that you feel sorry for. Siamese cats or kittens that appear weak or lethargic are very likely to have underlying health issues. It may very well be that these health issues will not be able to be resolved.

Look out for signs of sickness, diarrhea, sticky eyes and stuffy nose. Directly ask the breeder or Animal Shelter if the cat or kitten has experienced any of these problems.

Once you have bought your new addition home, be sure to make an appointment with your veterinarian. It is important to have your cat registered and the vet will also be able to give him / her a medical check-up.

Choosing a Boy or Girl

This is a tricky issue as there are so many different opinions on the matter! Some owners prefer male Siamese cats stating that they tend to be more affectionate – other owners prefer females as they are more affectionate.

Overall, it is best to select your Siamese kitten or cat without too much reflection on their gender. Siamese cats tend to by incredibly loyal, sociable and affectionate regardless of gender – both boys and girls will be very attached to their carers and will spend the majority of their time with their human companions.

The choice between male or females ultimately depends on the personal past and current experiences of owners. It is fair to say though that gender actually has very little impact on the cat's personality.

It is far more likely that early socialization has a far greater influence – and how much time you can spend interacting and bonding with your Siamese.

However, what is important to mention, is neutering.

This is very important to do as soon as the kitten is old enough. In addition to avoiding any unwanted pregnancies (and related health problems), after neutering, your Siamese will generally be more relaxed and calm.

Note that even if you do wish to breed your Siamese, it is beneficial to wait until the kitten is at least two years old. This means that your female Siamese will need to go through 2 to 3 heat cycles before breeding her. Consequently, she will need to be kept isolated from any males that may be intact. Note that animals looking for a mate are surprisingly determined and pretty much always successful – they will venture much further from your backyard to seek out a mate than you would imagine!

One Siamese Cat or Double Trouble

Siamese cats are such sociable creatures, that they do, without doubt, enjoy having a companion at all times. Indeed, they tend to thrive in homes where they live with a playmate. Ideally this might be another Siamese cat – but they are inclined to get along with other pets too.

The Advantage of One Siamese Cat

The main advantage of keeping only one Siamese cat is the cost implications – very simply put, it will cost a great deal less to keep only one!

Expenses are not purely restricted to the initial outlay, it also has a huge impact on day-to-day care. Such costs include food, cat litter and linings, vaccinations, vitamins, medical expenses, carriers, beds and toys. Depending on your financial situation, keeping just one Siamese cat may be the sensible and practical option.

Furthermore, you will have double the trouble to manage and look after – two mischievous playmates so keen to explore that trouble never seems to be far away. Indeed, it may feel easier to manage looking after just one.

If you are available, you can concentrate all your love and attention on your one special companion. The important thing to consider is that Siamese cats crave company – they will enjoy that of another Siamese cat, human companions, or even that of a dog (or dogs). Refer to Chapter Nine where we look at introducing your Siamese to the rest of the household.

The Advantage of 'Double Trouble'

Without doubt, Siamese cats enjoy company – and two means that they have a playmate available at all times.

Siamese kittens and cats all love to play – and having another Siamese cat around will mean that there are endless opportunities for play, fun and games.

Play is a very important component for all cats, especially the highly intelligent Siamese cat. Play includes practicing hunting behaviors, developing motor skills, keeping fit and healthy, and learning about their environment.

By having another Siamese cat to play with, the opportunities for constant interaction and socialization tend to result in a cat that is happy and content – and ready to socialize with their humans whenever they are available.

If you are planning to keep your Siamese cat as an indoor pet, having a constant playmate will help to prevent boredom – the two cats will be able to stimulate each other.

With two Siamese cats, it will not be such an issue if you have a particularly busy period at work – or on days when you are simply busy around the house or need to be out.

Chapter Eight – The Costs of Siamese Cats

This Chapter is designed to help you prepare for your Siamese cat – including cost implications and making sure that you have the basic essentials ready.

Estimating the Costs

There are two key areas of expense when it comes to owning a pet – the initial expense of purchasing your Siamese cat – and the general costs incurred over a lifetime.

By combining these costs, you can start to estimate the cost of owning a Siamese cat.

One of the key points to consider when it comes to financial costs is whether you are going to keep one Siamese cat or two (as discussed in previous chapter).

- **Initial Expense** – The initial expense of owning a Siamese cat includes the actual purchase (or adoption fee), and primary vaccinations.
- **General Ongoing Expenses** – This will include food, toys, routine vet visits, booster vaccinations – and possible major medical costs.

Initial Expense

The first expense will be purchasing your Siamese cat – or paying an adoption fee.

The average price for a Siamese kitten is between $400 and $600. This is based on purchasing a Siamese kitten from a reputable breeder.

An alternative option is to adopt your Siamese cat from a Rescue Shelter. Adoption fees vary but tend to be between $75 and $200. While adoption fees do vary, they are always used to cover a variety of expenses and help to support the work of the Animal Shelter.

Adoption fees ordinarily include the following; a medical check-up, any necessary medical treatment; spaying/neutering; vaccinations; microchip and registration; treatment for fleas, ear-mites and worms; any necessary bloodwork; dental care – especially relevant in older cats.

General Ongoing Expense

- **Medical Costs** – The most expensive outlay for your Siamese cat will be medical costs. This is difficult to predict as cost will obviously depend on the medical problems your Siamese comes to encounter.

The average consultation with a vet generally costs between $50 to $400. As well as general health, your Siamese cat will also require dental care – again you can expect to pay between $50 to $400.

If you decide to supplement your Siamese cat's diet with vitamins, expect to pay around $100 over the course of a year.

Preventative medication for fleas and heartworms costs around $20 per month.

Additionally, you may end up paying for emergency medical treatment.

You may wish to consider paying for pet insurance which will cover some of your veterinary bills.

- **Cost of Food** – Much of the yearly budget for your Siamese cat will go towards their food.

  There are many different types of food available for cats – to fit every kind of budget. Remember that expensive cat food does not necessarily mean that it will be superior (see Chapter Eleven – Health and Wellbeing).

  As an example, a 22-pound of Purina One Complete cat food costs around $18.

  Some owners choose to feed their Siamese cats with specially formulated food which has been designed specifically for Siamese cats. A 6-pound pack of this can be purchased for around $30.

- **Toys and Accessories** – The cost of toys and accessories simply depends on you – how much you want to spend on your beloved friend!

  It is true to say that due to their high level of intelligence, Siamese cats do need a much greater need for stimulation. Indeed, it is especially important for all Siamese cats that are kept as indoor pets.

This is where toys and accessories are of vital importance. However, note that whilst toys are essential, we will give you some incredibly useful ideas on simple and inexpensive solutions. Toys and accessories do not need to be expensive at all (see Chapter Ten and the section on 'creating toys on a budget'.).

A scratch post for your Siamese will be of great value. This you can be extravagant with (if you like) as there are many fantastic designs available. But if your budget is a little tight, you can buy at basic one for a minimal price – and I will show you how to make your very own scratch post with very little financial outlay – see Chapter Ten and the section on 'Scratch Posts – a Necessity'.

As you can see, if you have a budget that allows for it, you can splash out on all sorts of toys and accessories – but if your budget is limited, don't worry, you can fulfil the needs of your Siamese by simply making your own and making use of recyclable materials. Your cat will not notice the difference, either way will work perfectly!

- **Cat Carrier–** A cat carrier will be an essential item that you will need from the day you bring your Siamese home. Most cat carriers cost somewhere between $20 and $40.

  Although this is an item that you may be able to borrow from friends and family, consider that it is something that you will need to use on a fairly regular basis – indeed, some trips to the vet will not be planned and you won't want the additional worry of sourcing a cat carrier that you can borrow.

Cost of Holiday Care

Whether you travel regularly or only occasionally, holiday care will be a necessary expense for your Siamese cat.

It may be that you have a friend or neighbor that is happy to help. But do consider that your Siamese cat craves company and attention – if you think that your friend will pop into your home just to quickly feed your feline friend, it may be better to put something more official into place. Your cat will want that attention that he / she is accustomed to receiving from you.

Options include either a boarding cattery or a cat sitter. Here your cat will be left with a carer who has the skills and experience to meet the needs of your Siamese cat.

The cost of a boarding cattery varies depending on length of stay, time of year, type of boarding and whereabouts in the country the boarding cattery is. It would certainly be worth your while to shop around as rates do vary. Charges tend to range from around $15 to $30 per day. Cats are charged individually but discounts are normally given for additional cats.

The price of cat sitters also varies considerably – mostly depending on what type of service the pet sitter offers. Find out ahead of time so you can make plans – financial and otherwise.

Chapter Nine – Practical Preparations

Getting the Essentials Ready

The following is a check list of all items you will need for your Siamese cat – this way you can be totally sure that you haven't forgotten anything. We all know how easy it is to sometimes forget the obvious! Knowing what you need to have ready will make for a smooth transition when you do bring your cat home for the first time.

Note that most of these items are per cat. They will not want to share food bowls or beds, etc.…

Two cat bowls – one for water and one for food

Cat Carrier with padding / bedding for extra comfort

Cat Bed

Food – mixture of wet and dry

I.D. Collar

Blanket

Toys – lots!

Scratch post

Litter Box (including cat litter, scoop and litter mat)

Grooming Tools (basic stainless-steel comb is sufficient)

Arrange initial check-up with veterinarian

Plan flea and deworming treatment

Siamese Proofing your Home!

Siamese cats are always lively and incredibly inquisitive. More than any other breed of cat, your home will need to be 'Siamese proofed'.

This is not only to protect your home and possessions – but also to guarantee the safety of your curious feline companion. Without sufficient preparations, your Siamese will end up getting knotted up in wires and blinds, knocking everything off the shelf, or will be tucking into an entire pack of treats that you had planned to give as occasional rewards.

Siamese cats are keen and determined explorers. They tend to love the puzzle of how a door opens or the challenge of undoing a latch or catch. The Siamese regard such feats as a challenge – and they tend to persist until they are successful. So, think carefully about the contents of each of your cupboards – is your cupboard safe for your Siamese to explore – and could they damage the contents?

The following preparations will go a long way to getting your home 'Siamese Proofed'. Of course, you will be able to make further adjustments according to the behavior, inclinations and interests of your Siamese cat.

- Use child safety locks on any cupboards that you do not want your Siamese to open-up. Think about the safety of your Siamese as well as any possible damage to the cupboard.
- Keep small items such as rubber bands, buttons, beads or tinsel out of the way as your Siamese could choke on them. This is especially important for kittens, but you do also need to be careful with cats.
- Place all electric cords out of reach where possible. Otherwise, secure them in cat proof tubing.

- Be aware that some of your household plants may to harmful to your Siamese.

These practical adaptions are something all owners should follow. But in addition to this, lots of stimulation and interaction with your Siamese will also prevent much destructive behavior. Have a look at Chapter Ten where we give you plenty of suggestions on how to keep your Siamese busy and occupied – even when you are not at home!

Planning for Holidays

When you are thinking about getting your Siamese, you may well not be thinking about taking a holiday. However, luckily for us, holidays come around soon enough!

This is an important issue as your beloved companion is solely reliant on you to arrange sufficient care while you are away. And the tricky thing about Siamese compared to other species of cat is that Siamese cats love you and your company so much – that they will not like to be left alone.

So, whereas another cat may be happy with an automatic cat feeder for a few days – or a neighbor briefly popping in, your Siamese will need a little more than that.

Chapter Nine – Practical Preparations

Easy and fine if you are in the fortunate situation to have family or friends that live nearby - <u>and</u> have some time to keep your Siamese company. Otherwise, you need to consider either cat boarding or a cat sitter.

Cat boarding can offer peace of mind while you are away. You can have a good look around the cattery before you book so you can decide if this is a suitable option. They really do vary in what they have to offer – some are relatively basic while others are more like a 5-star hotel for cats.

A cat sitter is somebody who comes to your home meaning that your cat can stay in the luxury of their own home.

Which is better between these two options ultimately depends on the personality of your Siamese – and your own personal choice.

A cat hotel may be preferable where the Siamese cat is particularly sociable and really dislikes being left on their own. Cats who are generally with their owners 24/7 may find it more difficult to adapt to being on their own for any length of time. In this case, your Siamese may be better in a facility where there are plenty of cats and company nearby.

A cat sitter may be the better option for Siamese cats who are independent but enjoy the comfort of being on their own.

One of the advantages is that there will be no travelling in the car – or being forced into the cat carrier. Homely cats tend to prefer to sleep in the same special spot each and every day. Such cats would benefit from staying at home with a cat sitter who can come and look after them. Additionally, there are very practical considerations that may help you decide – a cat sitter will help give your house that looked in feel – so people are less likely to notice that your property is empty.

Additionally, you can ask the cat sitter to bring in mail, open and close curtains / blinds, turn lights on / off. Cat sitters would also be able to water plants both indoors and out in your yard.

Preparing for a Smooth Transition

It will be a very exciting time when you bring your Siamese cat home for the first time. For your new addition though, remember that you and your home are completely alien. Your home will be a completely new environment full of unfamiliar scents and features. Their routine will have been broken and so this is likely to be a stressful time for them. As well as simply feeling stressed, anxiety can lead to medical problems that will need to be treated.

For a smooth transition, try and keep as much as possible the same for your new companion.

Find out from the Breeder or Animal Shelter what food your Siamese has been fed. Initially, it is extremely important to keep thing as familiar as possible. This will help to lessen the shock of moving home and make for a much smoother transition. So, if the brand the breeder has been feeding your kitten is not the one you would choose, use it for the first couple of months at least or until your Siamese seems settled and 'at home' in your house.

The same is true for cat litter. Continue using whatever type and brand your Siamese has been accustomed to. They will be able to tolerate changes fine but wait until they are comfortable in your home.

Since smell is so important to Siamese cats, ask the Breeder or Animal Shelter if you can take something home with you that will smell of your new cat. Indeed, cats rely on smell to learn about their environments – and will it is scent that ultimately determines whether they feel safe or in danger. Ask if you can take with you their cat bed - or a blanket that they are accustomed to. This will help make your new cat feel more secure as there will be a familiar scent in your home.

To further increase feelings of security, think about giving the Breeder or Animal Shelter something from your house that will smell of you. If this can be given to your cat several days before they return home with you, your scent (and that of your home) will already be a little familiar to them.

Organizing a Place of Retreat

In the early weeks, your Siamese may benefit from a quiet room / area where they can retreat knowing that they will not be disturbed. Your new addition may prefer to stay in their own room as the rest of the house may well feel too overwhelming.

This is especially true for houses with children or other pets. Where possible, allocate your new Siamese their own room, just while they are settling in.

In this room, provide your new addition with everything they need – food and water, a litter tray, bed and bedding, scratch post, and some toys. Guaranteed, your cat would also love a box they could hide in – or a high shelf that they could sit up on and watch the world below them.

Note that cat's do not like to eat, drink, toilet and sleep in the same space. So, you will need to set up the room in such a way that this is avoided. Make sure that beds, bowls and litter tray are a reasonable distance apart. Additionally, it would be wonderful if this quiet room could have a window (securely shut!) – so that your Siamese can have a nose at the outside world.

You may not want or be able to devote an entire room to your new addition – but a special and safe place of retreat will be an enormous help in settling in. Once your Siamese appears settled and confident with you, you can arrange all the resources you have for your Siamese around the house as you would like. This is purely a recommendation to aid settling in.

Keeping your Siamese Indoors or Outdoors?

This is a major topic of debate amongst Siamese cat lovers – and may be a difficult decision for you to make. This is a very personal decision and there is no right or wrong answer. You simply need to consider your personal situation and make the best decision you can based on that.

Outside Cats – The crucial advantage of allowing your cat to roam free outside is that there have more opportunities to behave naturally. For example, there will be plenty of scope for hunting – and endless opportunities for climbing.

By allowing your Siamese to follow natural instincts and behaviors, they are likely to be mentally challenged and stimulated. They are far less likely to feel bored or frustrated. This generally means that when they come inside, they feel content, calm and happy.

The outdoor lifestyle will also provide plenty of exercise opportunities. This makes obesity less likely – and also other weight related health issues.

The chance of destructive behaviors indoors is less likely when a cat is allowed free range of the outdoor world. Your cat will have many scratching opportunities and will have used up excess energy. The chance of inappropriate urination indoors is also reduced.

Siamese cats who have free access to the outside world have no need for a litter tray. This is great for pet owners – it is never great to have a litter tray within the house, not to mention the fact that cleaning it will be an extra and hugely unpopular chore!

Indoor Cats – There are some equally valid reasons that may make you decide to keep your Siamese indoors.

Your Siamese will not be at risk of being taken by other people.

An indoor life will mean that your Siamese cat is protected from any kind of road traffic accidents.

Your Siamese will not be able to fight with other neighborhood cats and so will avoid fighting injuries.

By keeping your Siamese indoors, they are less likely to become ill as a result of contact with other cats in the neighborhood – other cats could be carrying cat flu or Feline Leukemia Virus.

An indoor cat will not bring parasites into your home. Fleas are a real problem for cats and they can be quite difficult to get rid of.

Overall, there are many valid reasons for letting your Siamese roam outside – and many valid reasons for keeping them inside.

Whilst a cat that has open access to the outside world will gain much more stimulation, exercise opportunities and chances to behave naturally, they also encounter many more dangers. They face the risk of being stolen or knocked by a car – very real and dreadful dangers. They have a higher chance of becoming sick if they encounter another sick cat. As well as health implications of this, there will also be potentially higher veterinarian bills. Additionally, the outside world makes your Siamese far more prone to fleas and other parasites.

Indoor cats also face their own set of problems. They are far more likely to experience stress due to boredom and inactivity. Feelings of stress and frustration are often exhibited in the form of behavioral problems - such as spraying and scratching.

Indoor cats are also more prone to becoming obese – simply because they tend to laze around more in the absence of stimulation. Obesity comes with its own set of health-related problems.

And on a very practical level, owners have more work with indoor cats – more of a challenge to keep them busy and keeping the litter tray clean.

Chapter Ten – Introducing your Siamese Cat

As well as settling in your Siamese cat to your house, he / she will need to be introduced to the other members of your household. Indeed, you will need to plan and manage the moment when your Siamese meets your dog(s) or your other cat(s), or your child / children.

Introductions with your other Cat(s)

If you already have another cat in the house (Siamese or otherwise), introducing the new arrival can be difficult. However, with planning, preparation and patience, the outcome is much more likely to be successful – it may even be that your new Siamese will befriend your established cat.

However, if they are not able to form a bond together, both can experience stress and anxiety.

The way in which cats are introduced really affects their future relationships. It is important not to gloss over this and hope for the best – be sure to take the time to prepare and take the process very gradually. The length of the process varies – somewhere around one week to several months. It depends on the personalities of your two cats and how they respond to each other.

A place of safe retreat will be of absolute paramount importance when introducing a Siamese to a household with an established cat. Ensure that you provide a 'safe' room where your new arrival has everything they may possibly need – and definitely a hiding place in case they feel threatened or insecure.

- The first step is to create positive associations around the safe room where your new arrival is residing. Place food bowls on both sides of the door – where you offer some special food – maybe even treats. Do also offer regular food in their normal bowl as usual.

- The next step is to exchange scents so that the smell of both cats become familiar before actually meeting. Think about swapping their bedding. Maybe place the other cat's bedding near the food bowl of the other cat. You could use extra blankets so that you have enough scented bedding!

- Temporarily remove the new arrival from their 'safe' room and allow your established cat to sniff around in here for a while. They will be smelling the new cat and leaving their own scent. However, only remove the new cat from their safe room once they seem confident in their new surroundings – you will need to wait several days or even weeks before attempting this.

- Once any sign of aggression has subsided around the door of the new arrival, you are ready to try visual contact – this is where the two cats can seem each other but there will be no physical contact.

One idea is to put one of the cats inside a crate or pen – or use a door that is transparent or netted – or have a small crack in the door that the cats are too wide to pass through. Note that the crate must be viewed as a positive place for the cat to go – you don't want to force your cat in with feelings of anxiety.

If the cat inside the crate is displaying any kind of distress, place a towel over the crate so that they feel protected. Remove the other cat from the room – however be aware that a cat who feels frightened may attack you – try to encourage them out of the room instead of picking them up and carrying them out.

- Use this method (visual contact with no physical exchange) until both cats seem relaxed in each other's company.
- Providing neither cat displays any kind of aggressive behavior, they are now ready for physical contact – but you will need to supervise.
- During their first few interactions, ensure that there are plenty of special treats and toys available. Keeping both cats busy will help to prevent the cats from staring and intimidating each other.
- Never punish any cat – even when they are displaying aggressive behavior. Simply separate the cats. After all, any aggression is likely to arise out of feelings of anxiety and insecurity. And don't forget cats are

territorial so it is naturally difficult for them to accept newcomers – an unavoidable fact.

- When the cats have been together and have shown no sign of aggressive behavior, they are ready to be left unsupervised. However, restrict these periods to just a few short minutes initially. Make it as frequent as possible – but in short bursts.

- In time, when both cats are relaxed in each other's presence, leave the door to the 'safe' room open.

Introductions with your Dog(s)

Siamese cats and dogs have been known to form close relationships with each other. It helps that your Siamese will naturally and ordinarily be very outgoing and keen to make new friends!

For a good relationship, it is extremely important that the dog is not allowed to frighten the Siamese. This means that a careful and gradual introduction is essential – take things very slowly; after all there is no immediate rush.

- Quiet and Calm – obvious though this may sound, do choose a quiet time of the day. Make sure that everybody knows what is happening so that everyone in the house remains quiet.
- No rushing – it is important to allocate plenty of time for this first introduction. This will help you to feel calm – which influences how your pets are feeling too.
- Delay your Siamese from meeting your dog(s) for several days or even a week. During this time, keep your two pets in separate parts of the house – but allow then to visit the other part to have a sniff (and leave their own scent). The smell of each other will gradually become a familiar scent to them.
- As smell is so important to both cats and dogs, scent has a big part to play in introductions. Ensure that your new pet smells of home before even contemplating an introduction.
  Collect scents from your new pet by stroking their head with a soft cloth. Then wipe this cloth around the home – on furniture and floor spaces. This will help to mix and spread the scents.

You could also try swapping the bedding of your pets so that they have the opportunity of smelling each other before they actually meet.

Or simply stroke the dog and cat separately – and do not wash your hands in between. This will help to exchange their scents. You'll want to wash your hands afterwards though!

- Avoid any kind of chase. One solution is to use a large dog crate or a kitten pen for the initial introductions. This way the two animals can see each other without having any kind of physical contact – providing your Siamese with protection.

  Within the pen or crate, provide your pet with a hiding space. This way if they do feel frightened, they have a secure place to hide. This will help to minimize anxiety. If they are curious, they may well emerge to say hi – knowing that they have this place of safety to escape to if necessary.

- If possible, create a platform within the pen – to enable your cat to climb up to a higher location. This will help them to feel more secure. If you use a strong cardboard box as a place to hide, this can also serve as a 'viewing platform'.

- Place the cat pen or crate on a raised surface so that it is not on the floor.

Now you have everything ready and set in place for your introduction to commence. Place your Siamese in the pen /

large crate and invite your dog to come into the room. Give both pets an abundance of reassurance and attention.

Ensure that you keep your dog on the lead. This guarantees that you can control any kind of unforeseen interactions. Don't be tempted to take the lead off, even when things appear to be calm and going well – this can change quickly. Request that your dog sits quietly – and provide rewards such as treats and praise for remaining calm.

Don't worry about how long or brief the introduction is. If your dog seems to become excitable, simply take him / her out of the room and try the introduction again either later in the day or the following day.

Continue with these controlled interactions every day for a few days. When you see that both Siamese and dog are calm during their meetings, the time is right to allow your pets to meet without using the pen / crate.

- Ensure that there are plenty of hiding spaces available to your Siamese. He / she may want to hide behind furniture for a while – jump up high or hide inside a box. Choose a room where your Siamese has some options!
- Do still keep your dog on a lead. It is of upmost importance to prevent the dog chasing your Siamese – this will be profoundly damaging to their relationship and any bonds between them will be severely delayed.

- Give your dog plenty of praise and treats for being calm. Your dog will associate the Siamese with rewards – and a time to be on their best behavior!
- Once this set-up has proved successful over several days, give your pets the whole house – and don't worry about restricting them to the one room.
- Just give both Siamese and dog plenty of opportunity to avoid each other if that is what they want. Keep feeding, litter tray and sleeping areas separate so that they have the space to be on their own.

Incredibly important – don't leave your Siamese and dog together unattended until you are 100% sure that they will not fight or chase. This will undo any progress that they have already made.

Although this sounds like a lengthy process, it is very likely to be an enjoyable one. It is fascinating and exciting to see how they respond to each other. Providing you have a dog that is calm and well behaved, it is normally a very positive experience. In time, they can form a special bond together – and can make excellent companions and playmates for one another.

Introducing your Siamese to Young Children

Due to their bold personalities, Siamese cats usually get along with children very well. Getting to know each other will be a valuable and enriching experience for both your child and your Siamese cat. Indeed, children often have more free time to devote to playing with cats – and Siamese in particular, will love all the attention they can get.

Make sure that your child is comfortable and confident around cats before bringing your new addition home. If your child is wary of cats, try and take your child to a friend's house who has cats. Let your child spend some time getting to know the cat so that they can build up confidence.

Ensure that you teach your child appropriate behavior around the cat – show them how cats like to be stroked. Having pets is a great way to teach responsibility – consider letting your child help with feeding, playing and grooming.

Make sure your child knows that your new Siamese is not a toy. Point out the signs that your cat gives off when they no longer want to play – or when they want to be left on their own. Make sure your child knows not to wake a sleeping cat – obvious to us but not necessarily to a child.

It is ideal if you can keep the cat's 'room of retreat' free from children. This is especially important in the beginning, when your Siamese is settling down into their new home.

Indeed, like any other relationship, the connection between cat and child is two-way. You want both to feel comfortable with the other. It helps if both have some private space where the other can't go. Perhaps your child's bedroom could be off limits until your child wants the cat to come in and explore – and similarly the cat's room could be off limits to the child in the initial settling in period.

Chapter Eleven – Bonding with your Siamese

As Siamese cats are particularly intelligent - and always incredibly inquisitive - you will need to find ways to keep them busy, stimulated and challenged. This will help to reinforce the bond between you. The more activities you enjoy together, the deeper the bond will be.

This chapter is designed to help you think of activities and play ideas that will keep your Siamese occupied and challenged - and provide them with plenty of scope for thinking.

Siamese cats who are not stimulated and challenged will quickly come up with their own ideas on how to entertain themselves – which are usually quite destructive and negative.

Playing and interacting with your Siamese is crucially important to their happiness, health and wellbeing. Unlike some other breeds of cats, Siamese cats tend to want to spend as much time as possible with their human owners. Whilst they love cuddles and will be content following you around the house (while providing a continuous commentary on what you are doing!), they also crave entertainment – and attention in the form of play.

Indoor cats in particular are in need of games and toys that use up a of energy through exercise.

You will find that your Siamese will play with you for as long as possible. Try to provide at least half an hour every day – get the whole family involved and hopefully your cat will have even more playing time! After all, the more play the better.

Favorite Toys and Games

An excellent idea is to rotate your cat toys. This keeps them fresh and exciting. Just bring the favorite toys out for a short time each day. This way, favorite toys remain stimulating – and stay as a favorite. Toys that are left out all the time begin to lose their appeal and you will find that your Siamese quickly loses interest.

There are a whole variety of amazing toys on offer in stores and online. Have a look and try and select a variety of different toys.

- **Playing Fetch.** Many Siamese cats will love to play fetch – and teaching them how is quite straightforward. Simply throw your cats toy to the other side of the room. Suitable things to throw include catnip mice, soft ball, scrunched up balls of newspaper. Try out different things but remember it needs to be something your cat can carry in their mouth.

Chapter Eleven – Bonding with your Siamese

Your Siamese will feel stimulated by the fast movement and will chase after it. As soon as he / she picks it up, encourage them to bring it back.

When they bring it back offer lots of praise and maybe even a treat. Throw it again.

Most Siamese cats pick this game up relatively quickly and will seldom tire of it – this is a fantastic way to burn off steam and encourage exercise.

- **Ping Pong Entertainment.** Try throwing a ping pong ball up the stairs for your cat to chase up and down. This will be a source of never ending entertainment. Just remember to find the ping pong ball at the end of the game – don't leave it on the stairs ready to trip over later – never a good idea!

- **The Appeal of String.** Cats also love to chase string – especially if moved about and wiggled by a willing household member!

    Just remember to avoid leaving the string lying around after supervised play– if your Siamese decides to try and eat it, string can be seriously damaging to their digestive systems.

- **Scrunched up Paper Ball.** Cats tend to love the sound of crumpled / scrunched up paper. Throw and roll crumpled paper around the floor for your cat to chase, wrestle and catch. Just be careful that your Siamese doesn't chew or swallow any paper.
- **Fabulous Wand Toys.** Wand toys are universally popular. They really imitate pouncing on and catching prey.

  Wand toys are basically a stick with a feather, string or bell at the end. You can either purchase these at the store or easily make your own.

  Simply pull the toy at the end of the wand slowly away from your cat's view – and watch as your cat pounces after it.

Try and be imaginative to make the game even more challenging for your Siamese. For example, make the most of corners and pieces of furniture so you can hide the wand. Watch as your Siamese enthusiastically and tirelessly leaps about in the air to catch the feather!

- **Catnip Scented Bubble mix!** – Oh yes, this really is available – and you'll find your Siamese cat loves it! Simply use a bubble blower to send bubbles floating through your home. Your cat will be fascinated and mesmerized – if they can pop the bubble they will be rewarded with the appealing scent and taste of catnip – making this a hugely popular activity.

Creating Toys on a Budget

No matter how many toys you purchase from the store, your Siamese will be eager for more.

Financial savings are an obvious advantage of making toys yourself – indeed toys for your Siamese really do not need to be expensive.

Another huge and ultimately more important benefit is that the toys you design and make at home will have a very different play element to those that you can purchase from the store.

Indeed, you can provide something that is challenging for your cat – something that will keep them busy and occupied for a while. You can also incorporate food into your games – which is always guaranteed to be a roaring success!

And the brilliant thing is you don't need to be good at Art and Crafts – or Design and Technology – to be able to give something to your cat that they will truly love and will keep them absorbed and stimulated.

- **Paper Bags** – Cut off the handles (to prevent your cat getting their head trapped in the loop) and leave it sideways for your Siamese to explore. Rustle the bag about and gently touch the sides. Your beloved companion will be eager to pounce on it and dive right inside. Sometimes put toys or treats inside the bag for extra interest and stimulation.
- **Egg Cartons** – These are such a great treat for your Siamese! Simply pop a treat into each of the compartments. It will be a challenge for your Siamese to dig them out, providing them with something to think about. Some cats will simply tip the carton over – try and wedge it so that your cat can't spoil the game!
- **Scavenging for food** – Give your cat their meal by hiding their food all over the house (this only works with dried food of course). Your Siamese will have a

great time looking everywhere – be creative and try and hide some food in some high up spaces.

- **Paper Ball Surprise** – Scrunch up a piece of paper and hide a treat in the center. He / she will soon rip it apart – and find what you have hidden inside.
- **Cardboard Boxes** – Always an endless source of amusement – never throw away a cardboard box until your Siamese has had a few games with it!
- **Playing with Light** – Cats will enjoy chasing light reflections – especially if you can move it so that you can make the light reflections bounce around. However, be careful when using a laser as they can be damaging to cat's eyes. Also, cats will become frustrated after a short while – switch to a 'real' toy after a while so that they have something they can really catch and have a wrestle with.

Scratch Posts – a Necessity

Arguably one of the most frustrating behaviors of all cats (Siamese being no exception), is their insatiable desire to scratch everything available. This is completely natural behavior that you cannot, with the best will in the world, stop. Scratching comes from the cat's instinctive need to sharpen and clean their claws. The purpose is to remove the unnecessary layers which shed when scratching.

Whilst you cannot prevent your Siamese from scratching, you can certainly encourage them to scratch other things – and leave your furniture alone.

There are a huge variety of cat scratchers and cat scratching posts available in stores and online. These can be basic or elaborate depending on what you prefer and what suits your budget.

Another option is to make your own scratching post. You will need a piece of wood and some rope – although any rope will be fine, cats do especially love sisal rope. Wrap the rope very tightly around your piece of wood. The wood alone is not sufficient as a cat scratching post because there is a risk that your cat will damage their paws or claws while scratching the wood.

Be aware that you will need to position the cat scratcher so that it is high up. This is because cats stretch their muscles while scratching – so they will not benefit (or be inclined to use) a cat scratcher that is at floor level.

Once you have your cat scratchers in place, you will need a patient approach to encourage your Siamese to use the scratcher as opposed to the furniture. Punishing is not appropriate – this is very natural behavior and any form of punishment will simply be confusing.

This will be a learning process for your Siamese. When you see that they are scratching the furniture (or about to start), simply lift them and place next to the cat scratcher.

Additionally, offer a clear and positive response when see that your Siamese is using the cat scratcher. This demonstrates that this behavior is welcomed.

Using a cat spray is also extremely effective in tempting your beloved Siamese to the cat scratching post instead of the furniture.

These three approaches combined make an effective strategy and most owners find success. This is a learning process however and you will need to be patient. No cat will immediately stop scratching the furniture. If you feel frustrated with how slow the process is, make sure that you are offering plenty of treats to reward positive behavior – scratching on the scratch post.

However, if you find that your Siamese is still determined to use your furniture – or drapes, try using a keep off spray. Simply spray the furniture – or areas where your cat is inclined to scratch.

Taking Indoor Cats Outside

Many owners choose to keep their Siamese cats indoors. In addition to providing lots of play opportunities, try and find a way of taking your indoor cat outside to play on occasion.

When your Siamese is a kitten, teach them how to walk on a lead. This way, you will be able to take your cat for a walk – either around your backyard or further afield.

Another option is to provide an outdoor space that is completely cat proof – or consider building a cat run; somewhere they can explore outside in safety. If you feel that you lack the time or skills to cat proof the garden or build a cat run, there are companies that will be able to do it for you.

By giving your indoor Siamese some access to the outside environment, you will be hugely enriching their lives. And, by making access restricted in this way, you will still be avoiding many of the disadvantages that may have made you decide to keep your Siamese as an indoor cat.

Training your Siamese

Due to their high level of intelligence, you will be able to train your Siamese to perform some basic tricks.

Training will be enjoyable and rewarding for you as the owner – plus stimulating and challenging for your Siamese. Your Siamese will like nothing better than spending time with you – consequently training will be viewed as a very positive experience for your Siamese.

You will need some degree of patience, but it is so worth the effort. Most people find they have loads of fun in the training process, and it is another way to further bond with your cat.

Clicker Training

Clicker training is highly effective. It works with many animals, including cats. Clicker training basically works by marking good behaviors with the sound of the clicker and a treat. Your Siamese will come to associate the clicking sound with a treat. The clicker is much more effective than verbal praise as the clicking sound is fast and unique – it is a completely different sound to what they are used to hearing.

The following are some examples of tricks to get you started. Once you have accomplished these, I am sure you will enjoy thinking up your own tricks to teach your furry friend!

Chapter Eleven – Bonding with your Siamese

- **Touching a Target** – The target may be your hand or the end of a stick. This is a great trick to start with as it is simple and easy for your Siamese to do.

  When your Siamese touches your hand or a stick with their nose, make a clicking sound and give a treat.

  Once your Siamese is accustomed to this, move your hand or the stick further away so that she must get up and come to you. Keep offering rewards and try again and again.

  Eventually, your Siamese will perform this trick without the lure of the clicker – and you will not always have to provide a treat.

  Use the same commands during training – be consistent, either call their name or simply say 'come' every time. When they are very familiar with this, they will respond to your verbal command alone.

- **Teaching your Siamese to Sit** – Using the same techniques, you will be able to train your Siamese to sit.

  Simply hold the treat over your cat's head and move the treat backwards towards their tail. This will cause him / her to go into a sitting position.

  As soon as your Siamese is sitting, use the clicker and offer a treat.

  Throughout training, use the command 'sit'. This

will encourage her to 'sit' without using the clicker or the lure of the treat.

- **Instructing your Siamese to High Five** – This trick is an extension of the 'touching a target' trick.
  Hold a treat above your cat's head – but higher than he / she can reach with their nose. Your enthusiastic learner will soon realize that they need to lift a paw to touch your hand.
  As soon as they do this, use the clicker and reward with a treat.
  Throughout training, use the command 'high five'. Over time, they will know what 'high five' means.

- **Jump on Demand** - This trick is going to be more challenging and will take longer to teach. However, eventually, you can train your Siamese to jump onto a chair when you give the command to 'jump'.
  In the beginning, click and treat when your Siamese moves towards the chair or simply touches it with their paw. Once this behavior has become established, hold the treat over the chair and say 'jump'.
  Click and offer the reward as soon as they have jumped onto the chair.

- **Jump through a Hoop** – With daily training, it is possible to teach your Siamese to jump through a hoop! Impressive huh! Make use of the same target that you used for 'touching a target' – either your hand or a stick.

First, lead your cat to the hoop that you are holding. As he / she walks through the hoop, use your clicker and offer a treat. While training for this trick, say the word 'hoop' so that you develop association between the word hoop and going through it to get a reward. Initially, keep the hoop low to the ground and lead your Siamese through the hoop with the target (your hand or stick).

Once he / she starts going through the hoop quickly and with no hesitation, hold the hoop up higher so that he / she needs to jump to get through it.

This trick is very satisfying for both you and your cat. It encourages your Siamese to think, to be active and to exercise.

Although these tricks seem like fun, they are important in securing the bond between you and your Siamese. They provide an opportunity to do something together – your cat will be stimulated, challenged and encouraged to think. By providing treats, you are ensuring that all training is completely positive.

Always bear in mind that patience will be required. It will take lots of practice – but the process of learning is so positive that it is well worth it.

Very importantly, always keep lessons relatively short. Just make sure you do them daily so that you are reinforcing what you are teaching.

Housebreaking your Siamese Kitten

Whether or not you are planning to keep your Siamese as an indoor or outdoor cat, the first few weeks will be confined to indoors. This means that litter training is crucial.

It is most likely that the Breeder or Animal Shelter has already litter trained your kitten. However, the trauma of moving can sometimes cause a backward step in terms of litter training.

Be sure that you use the same cat litter and lining for the litter tray. By keeping everything the same, your kitten should get the same message that this is where they need to 'do their business'.

When your kitten is first settling in, it is more reassuring if they can be kept in one quiet room where they have access to everything they need. When your kitten begins to explore the rest of your home, provide a few more litter trays so that your kitten always has easy access to them.

Chapter Eleven – Bonding with your Siamese

Be sure that your kitten has a litter tray that has lower sides for easy access. Older cats will also need lower sides if and when mobility is restricted.

If your Siamese is still reluctant to use their litter tray, try offering a variety of substrates – grit, wood, sandy litter. This way you can see what they prefer.

Ensure that the litter tray is situated somewhere private and quiet – and well away from water and food.

You can provide the option of open and covered litter trays. If you don't wish to purchase a covered litter tray, consider making a cover with an upside down cardboard box – simply make an appropriately sized opening.

Hygiene and cleanliness will be important to your Siamese – remember their incredible sense of smell. Many cats are so fastidious that they not use a litter tray if they have already dirtied it. In this case, try and provide an extra litter tray. Some cats prefer one litter tray for urinating and another one for pooing.

Scoop the soiled litter out as soon as it has been used. Replace the whole litter tray completely once a week at least. Cats will be put off by a strong scent of disinfectant, so this is important to avoid. Wash the litter tray with a ten per cent solution of biological detergent – rinse well with near boiling water and dry thoroughly before refilling.

Also make sure that you are providing a sufficient layer of litter. Cats tend to use the litter tray and then like to cover and bury it with the cat litter.

If your kitten has an 'accident', mop it up with a piece of tissue. Then leave this in the litter tray. This will help signal to your kitten that the litter tray is the place to go.

Clean any 'accidents' thoroughly. Otherwise, these areas will be the 'place to go'. Simply wash thoroughly with the ten per cent biological solution. Make sure that you use a disposable cloth, so you don't mistakenly spread the scent around. Wash thoroughly and rinse with clean water and then dry.

If you notice your kitten sniffing at the floor, this is a sign that they need to use the toilet. Simply lift your kitten into the litter tray. Additionally, you can place your kitten in the litter tray after they have eaten – or when they have woken up as this is when it is likely that they need to 'go'.

Training Your Siamese to Walk with a Leash

Many owners who decide to keep their Siamese as an indoor cat will want to try and take their beloved companion for a walk around the backyard or around the neighborhood. If you have not cat proofed your backyard, then using a leash is a suitable option. This way your Siamese can enjoy the scents and movements of the outdoor worlds but will be kept safe by the restrictions imposed by using a leash.

Cat harnesses are available in stores and online. You can attach a lightweight cat leash to these harnesses with a secure clip. A collar is not sufficient as your cat could slip out of it. Ensure that the leash pulls on your cat's chest – and not their throat or neck.

An alternative to a harness is a walking jacket. Your Siamese will not be able to escape from a walking jacket. The leash is attached to the middle of the back. This prevents tugging anywhere near your cat's throat.

Preparing for Leash Training –

Chapter Eleven – Bonding with your Siamese

- Leave the harness and leash near to your cat's usual sleeping area. Over several days, the scent of the harness and leash will have become familiar to your Siamese.
- Put the harness on your Siamese. Make sure that there is enough room to slip two fingers between the harness and your cat's skin.
- Once the harness is on, give your cat a treat so that they feel reassured – plus plenty of praise.
- Try and leave the harness on while your Siamese is in the house. If they appear troubled by the harness, distract them with a favorite game or activity.
- When your Siamese appears to be accustomed to wearing the harness, take it off.
- Over the next few days, keep putting the harness on for short periods. Leave the harness on for longer periods each time.
- After a few tries at wearing the harness, attach the leash to the harness. Let your Siamese explore the house and follow her daily routine with the leash dragging along behind him / her. Don't leave your cat on their own with the leash attached – you need to watch out for any entanglement or getting caught up!
- Provide plenty of praise with the leash on – and offer some treats to eat.

Ready for Leash Training –

- After making the preparations for leash training, you are now ready to try the real thing!

- Start out inside; with your cat wearing the harness and the leash attached. This time, take hold of the end of the leash. Follow your Siamese around – let them choose where to go. Simply hold the leash very lightly – do not restrict any movements.

- Practice this for several days and gradually begin to guide your Siamese, pulling very lightly on the lead. However, make sure this remains a positive experience, if your Siamese seems unhappy in any way, let them guide you. If he / she tugs at the leash, stop straight away – try again when they are feeling relaxed.

- Once your Siamese is happy for you to use the leash and harness – and have you guide them around the home, you are ready to show the big wide world to your Siamese.

- Until your Siamese is accustomed to walking on a leash, stay within your own yard. Spend increasingly longer periods over time outside.

- Once your Siamese is very familiar with walking around your backyard, you could try venturing out to more public locations. However, your Siamese will be content to stay within your backyard – an exploration of the backyard will provide your Siamese with all the benefits of walking outside on a leash. It is entirely dependent on where you would like to go with your Siamese!

Chapter Twelve – Health and Well Being

Diet and Nutrition

As with any living creature, diet and nutrition is absolutely key to ensuring an active and happy life for your Siamese. Although you cannot eliminate all medical issues and problems, a good and balanced diet goes a long way in ensuring that your cat is the healthiest that it could be.

There are three types of food that are suitable for Siamese cats – dry food, wet food, and fresh food. A combination of these will guarantee a balanced and varied diet for your cat.

Ideally, your Siamese cat should consume a balanced, rich and varied diet. If your veterinarian detects any nutritional deficiencies in your Siamese, vitamin supplements are available.

You will see that there are advantages and disadvantages to both wet and dry food. Although this paints a confusing picture, remember that neither is right or wrong. As you will see, wet food appears better for urinary health and dry food appears better for thyroid health. Perhaps the ultimate solution is to consider what your cat prefers – and to offer a combination of wet and dry food.

Dry Food

- **Fantastically Convenient** and mess free, dry food can be left out all day for your Siamese to graze on.
- **No Impact on Dental Health -** For many years, it was believed that dry food was better for your cat's teeth.

    This opinion has generally been discarded on the basis that cat's do not naturally chew their food – they tear, shred and swallow whole. This means that food has very little impact on dental health. What is more important for dental health is genetics – and dental check-ups by the veterinarian.
- **Nutritionally Equal –** Dry cat food is often regarded as nutritionally inferior to wet cat food. In fact,

providing both are of good quality, they have the same nutritional value.

- **No Water Content** – Whilst wet and dry food are pretty much the same thing, the essential and critical difference is that the dry food has no water content. Vets universally agree that cats are healthier when they consume plenty of water – (see later section, Maintaining Good Hydration) – and wet food has more water. So, cats who consume mainly dry food will need to drink much more water. As cats are inclined to drink little water, many cats on a dry food only diet will be moderately dehydrated.

- **More Likely to Cause Obesity** – Since dry food is dense and has an extremely low water content, your cat is more likely to overeat when it comes to dried food. The water content in the wet food is likely to make your cat feel fuller. Additionally, the tendency with dried food is to leave it out all day. This is ideal for cats with a low appetite – but cats who enjoy their food have a greater opportunity to overindulge – and consume more calories than they are using.

- **Age Specific Dry Food Available** – As with all cat breeds, Siamese cats require different diets dependent on their age. For example, kittens need feed high in fat and protein to stimulate growth. Adult Siamese need a more balanced feed – around 25% protein, 40% fat plus fiber, vitamins and Omega-3 and 6. Older Siamese cats will need a diet that is not as high in protein and fat. Age specific foods meet the dietary requirements of your cat, so you can be sure that you are providing the most appropriate and nutritionally beneficial food.

Wet Food

- **Better for Hydration** - Water is essential for good health. Cats generally consume minimal amounts of water through drinking. Therefore wet food really helps as it means that your cat is obtaining water through their food. Wet food typically has 70 – 80% water content. In the wild, where cats gain most of the hydration through food, the prey that they eat would normally be about 60 – 70% water. So, in terms of water content, wet food is a good match to a cat's natural diet of prey.
- **Helps Avoid Urinary Tract Issues** – Good hydration, which is helped with a wet food diet, helps to prevent urinary tract problems and will be better for kidney health. Any cats that have health issues that affect their kidneys (including hyperthyroidism, diabetes and cancer) would probably benefit from a wet cat food diet.
- **More Suitable for Weight Loss** - The high water-content of the wet food means that your cat will

recognize when it is full more effectively. Additionally, wet food tends to be offered as part of a 3-meal diet (compared to dried food which tends to be left available at all times).

- **Easier to Consume** – Wet food may be easier for young kittens to consume. Indeed, wet cat food makes an easy transition from milk to solids as it is very easy to eat.

  Additionally, older cats who may have lost teeth – or who have dental problems – will find it much easier to consume wet food.

- **Hyperthyroidism** – Research has shown that there is a link between wet cat food and thyroid gland problems in cats. It is not known why but some scientists have inferred that it may be connected with the materials from the can. Thyroid problems are very serious in cats.

Fresh Food

Fresh food can be offered as a supplement to the diet of your Siamese. It will most certainly be thoroughly enjoyed and will provide a different range of nutritional benefits.

Suitable fresh foods include fish such as salmon, cod and hake. Check for bones in the fish. Also popular are cooked chicken or turkey.

Do not serve fresh food raw – you will need to cook them first.

Ideal Weight for your Siamese

Even though the Modern Siamese appears to be leaner and markedly slenderer than the Traditional Siamese, the ideal weight for both the Modern Siamese and the Traditional is actually the same.

Both the Modern and Traditional Siamese cat weigh between 2 and 4.5 kilograms (4.5 to 9lb).

Knowing the weight of your Siamese is important. This is because keeping to an appropriate weight will be one of the most effective ways to provide good health.

Obesity inevitably leads to countless health problems.

Maintaining Good Hydration

As well as thinking about the food you give your Siamese, also remember the importance of water. Indeed, water constitutes about 80% of a cat's body.

Clean and fresh water should be available always. This is absolutely critical for the health and well-being of your Siamese.

Also make sure that the water is easily available. It may be beneficial to provide more than one water bowl in the house. Easy access to water may encourage your cat to drink more water than if they had to always go to the kitchen for a drink.

If a cat does not consume sufficient water, he / she will become dehydrated. This effectively means that the cells in the body do not contain enough fluids to perform vital functions. Dehydration can cause kidney damage, heatstroke, shock and damage to the circulatory system. If dehydration is not treated, the cat could ultimately die.

Cats that do not consume adequate amounts of water are much more prone to urinary tract issues. Indoor cats, in particular neutered males, are very prone. Dehydration can cause urinary tract infections, kidney stones, feline idiopathic cystitis, and lower urinary tract disease.

The reason that cats in the wild drink little water is because they don't need to. They eat prey which is naturally high in water content – so the cat remains hydrated primarily through their food.

Note that any change in water consumption can be an indication of a health problem. Respond to such changes with an immediate visit to the veterinarian – early detection of illness can help enormously in subsequent treatment.

A cat with a urinary tract infection, kidney disease or diabetes will drink more water. A cat with liver disease or a respiratory illness will drink less water. Diarrhea, vomiting and fever will also cause a cat to drink more water.

Grooming

Siamese cats have smooth, sleek and short fur which sheds very little. This they keep very clean by grooming themselves on a regular basis. Their short, low shedding fur, and instinctive tendency to groom, means that they need very little help in the way of grooming.

Being such enormous attention lovers however, Siamese cats do tend to enjoy being groomed – and they may very well appreciate the sensation of it. Whilst you may find that it is a good way to bond and spend time together, grooming your Siamese will have very little impact on the appearance of their coat.

The most important influence on shiny and healthy-looking coats is to provide your Siamese with a good quality diet.

Cat malt may be given as a supplement to your cat's diet. Because cat's wash their coat by licking, hairballs can form in the stomach. These can cause vomiting and diarrhea. Cat malt helps to prevent the hairs from forming into a hairball. It benefits the natural passing of the swallowed hair and any other indigestible items through the digestive tract.

Common Medical Problems in Siamese Cats

Responsible Siamese cat breeders have worked hard to evolve a breed of Siamese that are strong and generally free from health problems. It is true to say that the more diverse the gene pool, the healthier the creature – therefore mixed breeds tend to be healthier.

- **Sensitivity to Anesthesia** – more than other breeds of cats, Siamese tend to be more sensitive to anesthesia. Some experience severe allergic reactions to the medications used for anesthesia. Your veterinarian will be aware of this trait and will be able to answer any questions you may have about the precautions you can take to minimize this risk.
- **Cross-Eyed** - or convergent strabismus was considered a normal trait for Siamese cats in the past. Today, most Siamese cats are not cross eyed although it is a far from rare condition as some still carry this gene.
A genetic flaw in their eye structure meant that Siamese cat's developed crossed eyes – to see straight ahead, they would need to cross their eyes. This genetic trait is the same trait that causes the point coloration in Siamese. Being cross eyed does not influence the cat's behavior in any way – nor does it affect vision.

- **Respiratory Problems** – Siamese cats tend to be more inclined to experience respiratory problems, especially as young cats. Upper Respiratory Infection (URI) is generally caused by one of two common pathogens.

  Calicivirus ordinarily lasts for one week. Symptoms include nasal or eye discharge, ulcers around the mouth and nose – and general lethargy, and extensive aches and pains.

  Feline rhinotracheitis lasts between 2 to 4 weeks where the cat will experience excessive sneezing and drooling.

  Most adult cats will be able to avoid URI if they receive up-to-date vaccinations. Cats that are kept indoors will also have further protection.

  Ensure that kittens are kept clear of drafts to lessen the chance of respiratory problems.

- **Psychogenic Alopecia** - this is a stress related condition wherein obsessive licking causes bald spots.

  Siamese cats are so sociable and intelligent that they will experience stress and unhappiness without adequate company and stimulation. Indeed, Siamese cats in particular, will not thrive in an Animal Shelter unless they can be provided with a lot of interaction and attention.

  Feelings of stress and anxiety often leads to this tendency to over-groom.

Boredom and anxiety stemming from change in environment (house move, new addition to family, problems with other cats) can also lead to this condition.

- **Vestibular Disease** – this is a genetic problem connected with the inner ear (specifically the nerves serving the ear) that effects some Siamese cats. Symptoms include loss of balance, disorientation or dizziness. Cats suffering with this will often tilt their head.

  Although this condition will often clear up without medical intervention, advise and a check-up with your veterinarian is advisable. If necessary, your vet can prescribe medication.

Life Span

Siamese cats tend to be fit, strong and healthy cats. They are inclined to live longer than some other cat breeds.

Their average lifespan tends to be between 15 and 20 years. Some have been known to live longer than this – but also some will not live for us long as the expected 15 years.

Due to the higher risks facing cats that can roam around outside, the life expectancy is longer for a cat that is kept indoors.

Chapter Twelve – Health and Well Being

Chapter Thirteen – To the Shows

Many owners of Siamese cats like to take them to shows. This can be a great way to meet other people who are also passionate about cats. You may prefer just to go to watch the cat shows but you may also enjoy 'showing' your precious Siamese.

It may be beneficial if you can attend your first show as a spectator. This way, you will know what is involved in showing your cat.

Cats entering a show will be evaluated and judged according to a written standard for their breed. The standard describes the ideal specimen for the breed – (note that this standard can be revised by members of the breed council). A breed standard enables judges to evaluate cats accurately and transparently.

Show listings are advertised several months in advance. You will find them in various cat publications. Also listed in the show schedule will be show locations, entry fees and contact details.

Note that you will need to complete an official entry form for each cat that you enter.

The Show Essentials

- **Excellent Health** – you will only be able to show your cat if they are in optimum health. No fleas, no ear mites, no discharge from eyes or nose, no bare patches of skin, no sniffles or sneezes.
- **Up-to-date Vaccinations** – all vaccinations must be up-to-date. Ensure that the vaccination certificate describes your cat correctly. It should include your cat's full name, correct breed, color, sex and age.
- **Cat Carrier** – You will need to transport your cat to and from the show in a pet / cat carrier.
- **Show Curtains** – These are used to line the inside of your cat's cage.

  The idea behind the curtains is to prevent cats from seeing each other – and so there is less likelihood of any verbal or physical aggression.

  The ideal curtains should be cut to fit to the size of the cage (find out cage size on the show announcement).

  Think about using curtains that will complement the coloring of your Siamese.
- **Show Cage** – These are provided at the show by the sponsoring club. The size of the cage varies in accordance to whereabouts in the country you are exhibiting. Find out the cage size from the show announcement.

- **Toys / Comforters** – Take your cat's favorite toy, pillow or bed that you think will help to make them feel comfortable and secure.

  The show will provide cat litter, but you may want to bring your cat's regular litter pan for familiarity. Similarly, the show is likely to provide food for your cat, but it may be beneficial to bring your own as you know what your cat likes.

- **Grooming Tools** – You may wish to bring your cat's comb or brush to perfect grooming immediately prior to the judging.

- **Claw Clipping** – The show rules require that claws should be clipped. Entry may be refused to cats' who have not had their claws clipped.

  When clipping claws, clip them as far down as possible without cutting the quick (this is the pink area near the base of the nail) – don't simply clip the extreme tip of the claw. You will need to clip claws on back feet as well as front.

  Always use proper clippers and ask your veterinarian for a claw clipping demonstration if you feel unsure.

What to Expect

Arrive at the show hall in plenty of time, as much as an hour before the official start of judging hours.

On arrival, check in with the entry clerk. You will be given a cage number and benching row. Find your cage and put the curtain into position as well as any toys, blankets, food and water bowls.

Make sure you check the judging schedule, so you don't miss any judging of your cat's class!

There will be spare time between judging where you will be able to go and look at other breeds and will have an opportunity to talk to the owners. If you are concerned about leaving your cat, ask your neighbor to watch after your cat. The people exhibiting at the shows are usually very friendly and keen to talk – you share a common passion after all.

Before entering your cat into a show, make sure you have read all the show rules – it is better to be aware of all the rules rather than accidentally break one of them!

Are Shows Right for my Cat?

The intention is that you and your Siamese will enjoy going to shows. If your cat is not happy at a show, then it is not advisable to take them.

Consider your cat's personality and think about whether you think they are suited to the 'show environment'. Cats that are shy and nervous will likely see a show as a negative experience. Luckily, Siamese cats tend to be confident and very friendly – this makes them well suited to shows.

If you own your Siamese as a kitten, this is the best time to take them. Younger cats are more receptive and accepting of new situations – if your cat is already accustomed to shows, then they will feel more relaxed and are far more likely to enjoy it.

Chapter Thirteen – To the Shows

Whilst extreme care is taken at shows to keep the risk of infection to an absolute minimum, contact with other cats means that there is a higher risk of encountering another cat who is ill.

Also, very importantly, if you are showing a pedigree cat, do find out if your cat meets the breeding standards and is good enough to be shown. This will hopefully avoid any disappointment on the day you turn up for the show.

If you are unsure whether your Siamese meets the breeding standards, seek advice from the breeder or any other cat lover experienced in cat shows. The Show Entry Clerk is also normally happy to offer advice.

Chapter Fourteen – Afterword

If you were wondering whether a Siamese cat is for you, I hope that this book has satisfied all your uncertainties. I am sure that other more experienced Siamese cat owners will have recognized the traits we have discussed – and have learnt lots of new things too.

Siamese cats are undeniably unique – so precious, graceful and intelligent. They do require more intense care than other cat breeds. And they most certainly thrive in an environment where love and attention are plentiful.

Whilst the care required may be too demanding for people who are away at work for long periods of time, for those of us who can spend the time to meet their needs – there surely isn't a more deserving creature. And, you will be repaid in unlimited and unreserved affection, 24 hours a day!

Your Siamese will be your Number One loyal companion. He / she will be at your side, interested in whatever you are doing - constantly. And your beloved companion will always have a lot to say to you – they will talk about whatever you are doing with their loud and distinctive voice. This is perfect if you are a person who likes to chat too!

Note that your Siamese will think they are far superior and more important than any other household member – but you will surely love them even more for this too!

This book will have given you the knowledge to meet the needs of this wondrous creature in the best possible way.

You are now ready to make practical preparations for the special day when you bring your new companion home. You know how to manage behavior and are ready to teach your eager learner some fabulous tricks. What's more we have given you lots of tips in how to keep your energetic friend busy and hopefully out of mischief!

I hope that my discussion on diet and nutrition will have helped form your opinion on what you think is the best diet for your cat. And you will be aware of common medical problems to look out for.

Chapter Fourteen – Afterword

And hopefully many of you will enjoy the fun – and razzle and dazzle of the Shows. Indeed, the shows are for everyone, both newcomers and highly experienced owners – welcome to all!

Glossary

A

ACFA – Refer to American Cat Fanciers' Association.

Acute Disease – A medical problem with rapid onset – and often a short duration. Such cases will need immediate medical care.

Adult Cat – A cat that is eight months or older is classified as an adult cat.

Alopecia – A bald area where there would ordinarily be hair.

Alter – A spayed or neutered cat.

American Cat Fanciers' Association - Beginning in 1955, the ACFA has grown to be one of the world's largest cat organizations. Their objective is to promote the welfare, education and knowledge of domesticated, purebred and non-purebred cats.

Any Other Color – Commonly referred to as AOC. This means a non-recognized color or pattern in a particular breed of cat.

B

Glossary

Benched – At a cat show, this refers to the area where the cat is kept and displayed while it is not being judged.

Best in Show – Most points and winner of a championship.

Best of Breed – A cat which is judged to come closest to meeting the breed standard among all other competing cats of that breed.

Blue-Cream - A mixture of blue (gray with a blue hue) and cream.

Blue-Cream Lynx Point – Color points that are a mixture of blue and cream with an underlying tabby pattern.

Blue Point – This describes the color of the coat – gray with a hint of blue.

Booster Vaccination – A further injection that is given after the primary injection. This continues immunity to certain diseases.

Breed – Cats who share common ancestors and who have similar physical characteristics.

C

Canadian Cat Association – Known as CCA. It includes a registry of purebred cats, show listings, show schedules and Canadian breeders.

Glossary

Carnivores – An animal that consumes primarily meat.

Carrier – A cat that carries a genetic defect or disease.

Castration – This is neutering for male cats where testicles are removed.

Cat Collar – Worn around the cat's neck. Useful to attach name tag.

Catnip – The Latin name is *Nepeta Cataria.* This is a plant that belongs to the mint family – which explains why catnip is also referred to as catmint. It acts as a hallucinogen to cats.

Cattery – Where cats are bred or boarded.

CCA –Refer to Canadian Cat Association.

Chocolate-Lynx Point – Medium chocolate brown coat with an underlying tabby pattern.

Chocolate-Tortie Point – Medium chocolate brown points that have an underlying tortoiseshell pattern.

Clowder – A group of cats is called a clowder. A group is defined as 3 cats or more.

Color Class – Cat Associations use these to classify certain coat colors or patterns, such as shaded colors of parti-color.
Color Point – The Siamese have a 'pointed' color pattern where the face, ears, tail, and legs are a darker color than

the body.

Cream – Can be described as a pale beige color. It is essentially a diluted version of red.

Cream – Lynx Point – Points that are cream to pale red with an underlying tabby pattern.

D

Dam – A mother cat.

Declawing – The surgical removal of claws. Cats that have been declawed are barred from entering competition shows.

Dehydration – The harmful reduction in the amount of water in the body.

Dilute – The paler version of a primary color. The dilute of black is blue and the dilute of red is cream.

Domestic – These include all nonpedigree cats.

E

Ear Mites – Minute insects that feed on the lining of the ear canal.

External Parasites – These include ticks and mites that affect the outside areas of the body.

F

Fawn – A pale beige color.

Felid – A wild cat belonging to the cat family.

Feline – A cat or member of the cat family.

Feline Leukemia Virus - One of the most infectious and lethal diseases found in cats.

Feline Lower Urinary Tract Disease – Often referred to as FLUTD. This urinary tract disease causes urethral blockage and kidney stone formation.

Feline Urologic Syndrome – FUS. This is a disease of the urinary tract causes blockage of the urethra in male cats. It can be fatal.

Feral Cat – These are cats that live outdoors and have little or no human contact. Feral cats do not usually allow humans to touch them or handle them in any way – but some may make attachments to people who regularly feed them.

Fever – A temperature in cats that exceeds 102 degrees.

G

Glossary

Genes – Controlling growth, development and the physical characteristics of the cat, genes are found in specific locations on a chromosome.

Gestation – The refers to the period of pregnancy. The gestation period for cats is between 63 and 69 days.

H

Household Pet – These can be domestic or purebred cats but who are not registered. There are special categories for household pets in cat shows.

Hybrid – Different breeds of cat (two or more breeds) that mate together create a hybrid.

I

Inherited – Characteristics which are the outcome of genetics.

Internal Parasites – Organisms such as larvae and worms that live and feed on their host in the intestinal tract.

J

Jacobson's Organ – A sensory organ situated at the top of the cat's mouth which is responsible for smell and taste.

Glossary

Judging Cage – Cages in the judging area.

K

Kindle – A group of 3 or more kittens are sometimes referred to as a kindle. This is an alternative word to a litter of kittens.

Kitten – A cat that is younger than 8 months.

L

Lavender – A coat that is gray with a pinkish hue.

Lilac Point – Gray color with a pinkish tint.

Lilac – Cream Point – A mixture of lilac and cream.

Lilac – Cream Lynx Point – Points that are a combination of lilac and cream with an underlying tabby pattern.

Lilac Lynx Point – Gray points that have a pinkish hue and an underlying tabby pattern.

Litter – Kittens who are born by the same mother at the same time.

Litter – The absorbent material used in a cat's litter tray / box.

Lynx Points – Color points that have an underlying tabby pattern.

M

Mask – Darker colored area on the face of the cat.

Meezer - Nickname for Siamese cats.

Melanin – Dark pigment which is produced by the body. This is what gives color to skin, hair, and eyes.

Microchipping – This enables cats to be identified so if they get lost they can be reunited with their owner. The chip is about the size of a grain of rice. It is positioned between the cat's shoulder blades.

Modified Wedge – Head shape that is triangular but not as extreme as a wedge.

N

Natural Breed – A breed that has not had the interference of selective breeding.

Neutering –Surgical procedure which prevents your cat from reproducing. Neutering is generally recommended at around 4 months.

O

Odd Eyed – Where eyes are of a different color.

P

Parasite – An organism that lives off its host – drinking blood or living in the digestive tract.

Pathogen – An organism that may cause disease.

Pedigree – These cats have been bred specifically to exhibit certain physical characteristics and breed related behaviors (for example Siamese cats are very 'talkative' in comparison to some other breeds).

Pigment – Coloration.

Pointed – A coat pattern where the body is paler than contrasting darker colors on the face, ears, tail and legs.

Points – The darker colored areas on a cat with a pointed coat.

Purebred – A cat who has ancestors of the same breed – or from allowable outcrosses.

Q

Queen – An unaltered female cat is sometimes referred to as a queen.

Quick – A vein that runs through a cat's claw.

R

Red-Lynx Point – Color points that are reddish / orange in color with underlying tabby pattern.

Renal - Medical issues connected to the kidneys.

Ringworm – Fungus causing contagious skin disease.

S

Seal-Lynx Point – Dark, almost black points, with an underlying tabby pattern.

Seal Point – Dark points, almost black.

Seal-Tortie Lynx Point – Dark points, almost black with a tortoiseshell coloring and underlying tabby pattern.

Seal-Tortie Point – Dark Points with an underlying tortoiseshell color pattern.

Selective Breeding – Deliberate mating of two cats with the purpose of achieving a specific trait – or eliminating a specific trait.

Show Cat – When a cat is judged to be top of its breed, it is known as a show cat.

Siam – Siamese cats originated from Thailand, formerly

known as Siam.

Sire – Father of a kitten

Spaying – This is the female specific term for neutering.

Stud – A breeding male cat.

T

Tabby – Coat pattern that is mottled or streaked with dark stripes.

Tamra Maew – Book of cat poems which included very early descriptions of the Siamese cat.

Thailand – Siamese cats originated in Thailand which was then known as Siam.

Tortie – Also called tortoiseshell. The coat colors are cream, red, and black mixed together.

Tortie Point – Color points that include a tortoiseshell color pattern.

Tomcat – This is a male who is unaltered.

V

Vaccinations - Help to prevent viruses and illness. It is recommended that cats are vaccinated every year.

Glossary

Variety – A cat that has registered parents but is not eligible for championship status because it does not conform to the breed standard.

Vibrissae – Collection of special whiskers which are used as a touch organ.

W

Wedge – Head type that has triangular shaped dimensions.

White – Cat color that lacks pigmentation.

Wichienmaat – The name for Siamese cats in Thailand.

Z

Zoonosis – Cat disease that can be contracted by humans.

Index

Index

Index